GRANDE TRAVERSE
AND THE MONT BLANC TOUR

GRANDE TRAVERSE

AND THE MONT BLANC TOUR

MALCOLM AND NICOLE PARKER

*A guide to classic skiing and walking routes
through the French Alps*

DIADEM BOOKS   LONDON
1986

Published in Great Britain by
Diadem Books Ltd., London

Copyright © 1986 by Malcolm and Nicole Parker

All trade enquiries to
Cordee, 3a De Montfort Street, Leicester

ISBN 0-906371-81-3

Colour separations by
Arneg Glasgow

Produced by The Ernest Press, Glasgow

Printed by
Brown, Son & Ferguson, Glasgow

INTRODUCTION

In the last ten years continental mountaineers have traversed the Western Alps from Lake Geneva to the Mediterranean, by walking in the summer and by skiing in the winter. The walkers follow the alpine section of the GR5, a long distance footpath linking Holland to the Côte d'Azur. This itinerary, with its variations (GR52 and GR55), is known as the *Grande Traversée des Alpes* (the GTA) and was conceived and way-marked by the GTA Association in 1971. The skiers follow what is now generally accepted by continental mountaineers as a basic route, sometimes choosing variants according to the party and prevailing conditions. Both traverses require a month in the mountains.

Either traverse is a complete mountaineering experience among diverse massifs, some prestigious like the Mont Blanc range, some little-known and unfrequented like the Ubaye. The routes described can take one from high altitude huts to decrepit barns and from traditional mountain villages to sophisticated resorts; for wilderness campers there is the addition of an exciting flavour of uncertainty and self-reliance.

The Winter Traverse demands the ability to cope with a variety of situations, some of which can be serious. For example prodding blindly in a blizzard to avoid hidden crevasses at 3600m requires much higher levels of competence and self-confidence than does skinning up a gentle slope of crisp snow. The Summer Traverse does not require the same high level of mountaineering skill, although hopping over slippery boulders at 2700m is certainly more demanding than walking across sunny Alpine pastures.

The third part of this book comprises the Mont Blanc Tour. No survey of the French Alps would be considered complete without its inclusion, since it forms the classic summer alpine walking tour.

In order to make the traverses and the Tour as safe as possible, parties should be physically fit, competent in map reading, suitably equipped and well-versed in mountain safety. More detailed information on the skills demanded for the traverses (on equipment, level of competence etc.) can be found in the respective intro-ductions to the summer and winter route descriptions.

The route descriptions have been split up into sections, four for the Winter Traverse and five for the Summer Traverse. Each section is further divided into 32 and 36 numbered sub-sections respectively. These represent a reasonable day's skiing or walking. For parties wishing to lengthen or shorten these, reference must be made to the Accommodation section. Alternative routes from the main described line, mostly related to difficult sections of the Winter Traverse, are indicated by the appropriate day number followed by a suffix letter – e.g. 5a. Local transport notes are included in the text when they are considered to be of use. The route summary at the beginning of each section of the traverse is given so that it can be followed on the relevant map prior to reading the description. Details on mountain rescue and weather reports are also included. Margin notes are added to draw attention to certain difficulties or characteristics of the route or to make general observations. The above comments also apply to the Mont Blanc Tour description, which has been split directly into day sub-sections.

The entries in the Accommodation section (Appendix 4) are numbered sequentially, and these numbers are cross-referenced in the text in brackets after the location. Accommodation actually on route is indicated by a bracketed reference number in normal typeface, whereas accommodation off route is indicated by italic typeface after the nearest location.

Abbreviations

D/R	Didier-Richard	PNV	Parc National de la Vanoise
CAF	Club Alpin Francais	MBT	Mont Blanc Tour
CAI	Club Alpin Italien	I	Italy
CAS	Club Alpin Suisse	Sz	Switzerland

GRANDE TRAVERSEE DES ALPES

The *Grande Traversée des Alpes* is the name given to both a high altitude walking route between Lake Geneva and the Mediterranean, and the Association which pieced it together.

Formed in 1971, the Association assumed the task of equipping the walking and ski traverses of the French Alps, with three objectives in mind:

★ to allow a maximum number of mountaineers to walk the Alps on a waymarked path, with hostels (*gîtes d'étapes*) distanced one day's walking from each other;
★ to protect the natural and cultural inheritance of the mountain population;
★ to contribute to the economic progress of areas suffering from the decline in agricultural activity.

In the last few years, skiers and walkers, and the inhabitants of the villages *en route* have come to know, or at least have heard of, the GTA. In order to spread information, the GTA created CIMES (The Mountain and Footpath Information Centre). You can obtain full information on mountain leisure activities, as well as a catalogue of the holidays and courses organised, by contacting:

CIMES – GTA
Maison du Tourisme,
14, Rue de la République,
38000 Grenoble, France
Tel. 76.54.34.36   Telex: 980.718

AUTHORS' NOTE An attempt has been made in this guide-book to describe two feasible traverses of the Western Alps and also the Mont Blanc Tour. The information within is based on first hand experience and numerous documents, the former being subjective and the latter proving sometimes to be erroneous.

In order to keep this book up to date it would be valuable that the parties completing parts of, or the whole of, the traverses send their comments and criticisms to the authors: c/o Diadem Books, 3a De Montfort Street, Leicester.

It is hoped that firstly, this work will allow British mountaineers to get to know the Alps as a whole and subsequently be more active in the lesser known areas; and secondly that, the extent to which so many Alpine areas have been desecrated become more widely known so that the same is avoided in the British mountains.

Malcolm and Nicole Parker
Le Bar sur Loup, France

ACKNOWLEDGEMENTS We would like to thank Henri Ménardo (photos 24, 25 and 27), Philippe and Brigitte Turco (photos 19, 22 and 26), Daniel Gastaldi, Peter Cornish and CIMES for the kind use of their photographs for illustration. Our thanks are also due to Don Sargeant, who has produced the maps and to Bob Moulton who has patiently edited the typescripts. Finally, we would also like to thank Bernard Gobbi for his advice and help.

Uncredited photographs were taken by the authors.

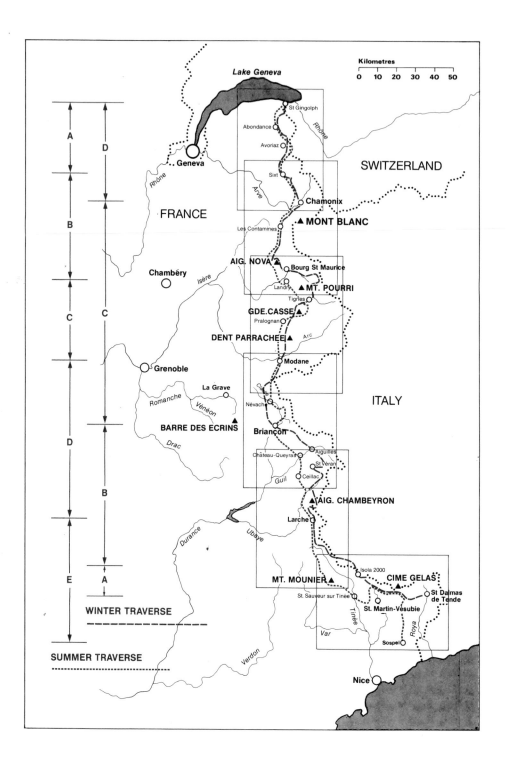

Kilometres

0   10   20   30   40   50

Lake Geneva

St Gingolph

Abondance

Avoriaz

Geneva

SWITZERLAND

Rhône

Rhône

Arve

Sixt

Chamonix

FRANCE

Les Contamines

▲ **MONT BLANC**

Chambéry

Isère

AIG. NOVA ▲

Bourg St Maurice

Landry

▲ **MT. POURRI**

Tignes

GDE.CASSE ▲

Pralognan

DENT PARRACHEE ▲

Arc

Grenoble

Modane

ITALY

La Grave

Romanche

Vénéon

Névache

▲

BARRE DES ECRINS

Briançon

Drac

Aiguilles

Château-Queyras

St Véran

Ceillac

Guil

▲ **AIG. CHAMBEYRON**

Larche

Durance

Ubaye

Isola 2000

CIME GELAS ▲

MT. MOUNIER ▲

St. Sauveur sur Tinée

St Dalmas
de Tende

St. Martin-Vésubie

Tinée

Roya

Var

Sospel

Verdon

Nice

A

B

C

D

E

D

C

B

A

WINTER TRAVERSE

- - - - - - - - - - - - -

SUMMER TRAVERSE

· · · · · · · · · · · ·

THE WINTER TRAVERSE

INTRODUCTION

It is too subjective to determine which is the best ski-mountaineering traverse of the Western Alps, but the most interesting itinerary is probably to follow the Franco-Italian frontier ridge as much as possible. This route is described from south to north because it is better, for safety reasons, to ascend south-facing slopes early in the day and to descend the less capricious northern slopes later in the day, besides which the downhill skiing is better in this direction. The fine Mediterranean weather in the southern sections should allow the skiers to get out every day thus training them for more hostile conditions further north. The whole route, starting at St. Dalmas de Tende fifty miles north of Nice, has been split into four sections with breaks at Isola 2000, Briançon and Chamonix, and finishing at St. Gingolph.

The massifs that are traversed provide varied ski-mountaineering: the unfrequented valleys, huts and ridges of the Mercantour massif, where it can be necessary to carry up to five days food, and the savage remoteness of the Ubaye provide thrilling ski-mountaineering. Further north, after the gentler relief of the Queyras and Briançonnais, the Vanoise (Graians) is objectively more serious with its crevassed high altitude glaciers, though paradoxically it is more frequented with numerous huts facilitating access. This traverse is particularly rewarding with its approach to the Mont Blanc range. Equally rewarding is the traverse of the friendly-looking Beaufortain massif, where one should not underestimate the avalanche risk. The shops, bars, discos and pistes of Chamonix are then left behind for the committing traverse to Sixt and the more hospitable Faucigny, which has unfortunately been infringed upon by large piste networks. The traverse ends with skiing across the picture postcard scenery of the Chablais to within a mile of the southern shore of Lake Geneva.

The Winter Traverse is a complete mountaineering experience, requiring judgement, alpine experience, skiing competence, stamina and luck. The rewards are unforgettable.

Only a very lucky party will complete the traverse in one attempt and it is realistic to assume that the traverse will have to be done over a period of at least two seasons. The fine weather found in sections A and B allows progress to be made relatively easily but the nearer the party gets to the Mont Blanc range, the higher the possibilities are of being blocked for days. The converse is, of course, possible so the time required will depend on the season.

The size of the party is of the utmost importance. The undoubted safety margin of a large party is partly offset by the sacrifice of speed, which itself contributes to safety. However, a small party, whilst much quicker, has a smaller safety margin, and this may be significant in the event of an avalanche accident. The optimum size is considered to be from four to six, and 300 metres of ascent per hour should be regarded as satisfactory.

The ski-mountaineering season begins as soon as the necessary snow has fallen, sometimes as early as November, and will usually continue until late June. Section D is probably best visited in mid-winter when its limited relief and its accessibility makes it reasonably safe from avalanche danger, whereas March, April and May are the best months for the higher sections.

In addition to this guide it will be necessary to use the definitive maps, which can be regarded as accurate.

Individual Competence

Skiers must be able to stem-turn in all types of snow, use ice-axe and crampons and be proficient in crevasse rescue for the traverse of the Vanoise (Section C). For those new to the mountaineering aspects of skiing, such skills can be acquired by attending a suitable course at one of the National Mountaineering Centres or by hiring a guide for a few days.

Specialist Equipment

The amount of personal equipment required will vary with the individual but it must be light and warm. Expected weather conditions will never be predominantly wet but they will be variable, sometimes extreme, so this must be taken into account. Less weight can be carried by sleeping and eating in huts but this is not always possible and it is necessary to allow for the possibility of having to spend a night in the open. The following list is a compromise and acts only as a guide:

Alpine climbing sac, karrimat, sleeping bag, ice-axe, crampons, head-lamp, ski-crampons, skins, improvised self-rescue gear, avalanche radio transmitter 'peips' (see note), salopettes, cagoule, long-johns, cotton T-shirt, down or gore-tex jacket, balaclava, woollen socks, woollen shirt, sun-hat, gaiters, woollen jersey, sun-glasses, silk gloves, woollen mitts, over-mitts, silk scarf. *(Note:* The peips transmitter is widely used in the French Alps and it therefore seems wise to carry the same equipment. Advice on skis, bindings, poles, skins and peips can be obtained from a specialist shop.)

In addition the following items should be carried by the party:

Maps, compass, altimeter, tent, cooking essentials (stove, pans etc), spare skins, adhesive, ropes – 35m of 9mm perlon (for each party of three), 2 ice-screws (for each party of three), snow shovel, first-aid, small tools. *(Note:* Gaz canisters often need to be heated to obtain the required flame.)

Avalanche Risk Assessment Service

The French authorities have an excellent avalanche risk assessment service which is of great help: See telephone numbers at the beginning of each section.

THE HIGH LEVEL ROUTE OF THE MERCANTOUR MASSIF
(Les Mesches – Isola 2000)

This section provides captivating alpine scenery at moderate altitudes between 2000 metres and 3000 metres. Only during weekends is the area frequented, so the pleasures of self-dependence and isolation are savoured. Additional summits can be climbed en route, from which Corsica, the Cote d'Azur and the Alpine chain are clearly visible.

Route Summary
Les Mesches – Baisse de Valmasque – Baisse de Basto – Cime du Gélas des Pas – des Ladres – Col de Salese – Baisse de la Lause – Baisse du Druos – Isola 2000.

Mountain Rescue
St. Martin de Vésubie Gendarmerie Tel. 93.03.20.10

Avalanche Risk Assessment and Weather Reports
Nice Airport Meteorological Office Tel. 93.83.17.24
Recorded Snow Report Tel. 93.71.01.21

Hut Information
Theoretically, each CAF hut has a wing of the building left open in winter, but it is advisable to carry the required keys. Obtaining them provides a major problem, but they are available and it is best to get them in advance from the Nice section of the CAF. A deposit must be left, and to avoid all problems of reciprocal rights it is best if one of the party is a CAF member. Contact: Club Alpin Français, Séction des Alpes Maritimes, 15 Avenue Jean-Médecin, 06 Nice. Tel. 93.87.95.41.

Day 1 From Les Mesches (65 and see Appendix 1 – Transport notes), follow the Vallon de la Minière to Pointe 1777m. Do not be tempted south (exposed to avalanches) but take a steep section on the right bank of the stream, which leads to Lac Saorgine and the Merveilles Hut (56).

The south-east shoulder of Mont Bégo (2762m) provides a superb descent.

Beware! The steep slopes require great respect and stable snow.

Day 2 From the bottom of the Vallée des Merveilles go nor-nor-west to a short steep slope and the Baisse de Valmasque (2549m). Descend north to the Lac du Basto, contour its left bank (west) until level with the middle of the lake, and climb a steep slope north-west to the Baisse de Basto (2693m). Descend a steep and narrow couloir on the north-west into the Vallon des Chamineyes and follow it to the Lac Niré. Join the Vallon de la Fous to the north-west and the Nice Hut (67), situated on a promontory dominating the Lac de la Fous.

The D/R red line from the Baisse de Valmasque to the Baisse du Basto is best ignored.

Mt. Clapier (3045m) provides a fine descent but care must be taken on the ascent after heavy snow, two skiers were killed in an avalanche in winter 1983.

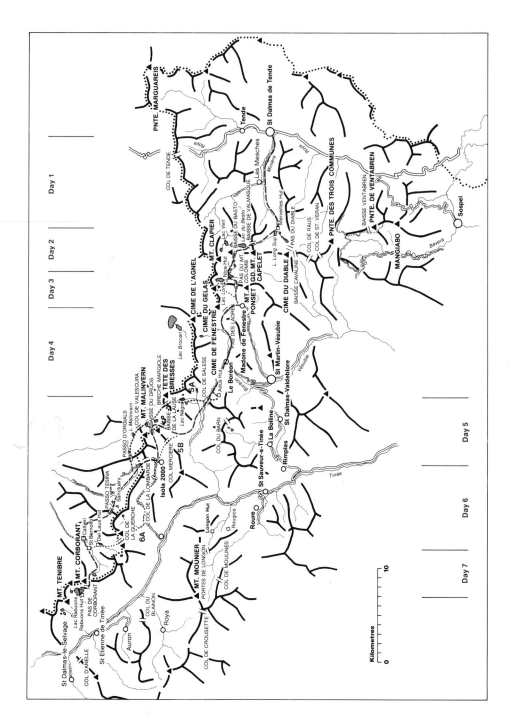

Day 1   Day 2   Day 3   Day 4   Day 5   Day 6   Day 7

PNTE. MARGUAREIS

Col de Tende

Tende

St Dalmas de Tende

Les Mesches

Roya

Minière

Roya

BAISSE VENTABREN

PNTE. DE VENTABREN

PNTE. DES TROIS COMMUNES

MANGIABO

Bévéra

Sospel

MT. CLAPIER

Lac Vert

BAISSE DU BASTO

BAISSE DE VALMASQUE

Lac du Basto

Merveilles Hut

L. Long Sup.

Lac Long

Nice Hut

PAS DU MT. COLOMB

PAS DU DIABLE

COL DE RAUS

COL DE ST. VÉRAN

BAISSE CAVALINE

CIME DE L'AGNEL

CIME DU GELAS

CIME DE FENESTRE

MT. COLOMB

GD. MT. CAPELET

PONSET

CIME DU DIABLE

PAS DES LADRES

Madone de Fenestre

Le Boréon

St Martin-Vésubie

Vésubie

St Dalmas-Valdeblore

Cougourde Hut

La Bolline

Rimplas

St Sauveur-s-Tinée

Roure

Tinée

Lac Brocan

Lac Nègre

COL DE SALÈSE

COL DES LADRES

Madone Hut

Bórgon

COL DU BARN

Longon Hut

MT. MOUNIER

PORTES DE LONGON

COL DE MOULINES

Rougios

COL DE CROUSETTE

COL DE BLAINON

Roya

PASSO D'ORGIALS

Malinvern

COL DE VALESCURA

BAISSE DU DRUOS

MT. MALINVERN

BRÈCHE MARGIOLE

TÊTE DES BRESSES

BAISSÉ DE LA LAUSE

5A

5B

COL MERCIÈRE

COL DE LA LOMBARDE

Isola 2000

6A   6B

COL DE LA GUERCHE

PASSO TESINA

PAS DE CORBORANT

Sanctuary

St Bernolfy

Cailleri

Del Laus Hut

Rabuons Hut

Lac Rabuons

PAS DE CORBORANT

MT. CORBORANT

MT. TÉNIBRE

St Dalmas-le-Selvage

COL D'ANELLE

St Etienne de Tinée

Auron

Roya

Kilomètres

0   10

Day 3   There are two possibilities for continuing:

(a) In excellent snow conditions: contour the north shore of the Lac de la Fous and follow the steep cwm to the north-west. Keep left of the course of the stream until Lac Long is reached. Two thirds of the way along the west shore climb a steep cwm nor-nor-west to around 2700m. Turn south-west to get above the big crags which dominate Lac Long and join the ridge north of the Cime Cabret at the best point. Climb easily north-west to beneath the east couloir of the Cime du Gélas, leave the skis and climb it to the summit (3143m). Back at the skis, descend sou-sou-west down the valley to Lac Cabret, contour it and find the way through small crags to join the valley, which leads towards the Madone de Fenestre Hut (54).

One of the best views of the Alpine chain can be seen from the top of the Gélas.

(b) In mediocre snow conditions: from the Nice Hut contour the Lac de la Fous by its east shore to around 2180m beneath the dam. Climb west-nor-west to about 2400m and finally more steeply to the Pas de Mt. Colomb (2548m). Descend south-west to the Madone de Fenestre Hut (54).

Wild, wild stuff.

Day 4   From the hamlet climb easily nor-nor-east then north-west to the Pas des Ladres (2448m). Descend (steep at first) west then north-west to the Lacs de Trécoulpes, then into the Vallon de Ht. Boréon at 1900m. Follow the Boréon valley south-west past a large *vacherie* to the cross-country pistes and to the *foyer de ski de fond*, which is above the road and lake. Skin up the road (19) towards the Col de Salèse (2031m) (passing in front of the Salèse Hut (97) by a short-cut), where a wild camp pitch can be made.

The cime W de Fenestre (2662m), the summit nor-nor-east of the Pas des Ladres, gives a short mixed ascent with fine views.

The outlet stream of the Lac de Trécoulpes makes a steep and narrow powder descent.

Day 5   A problem ensues: the best route from here is Variant 5a which is serious, taxing and committing. Two other possibilities exist: an easy route via Col Mercière and the following compromise. From the Col de Salèse join the Pont d'Ingolf by a forest traverse to the north-west. Follow an excellent near horizontal path, with fine views, north-west to the Vallon de Tavels, which is followed north until it joins the Vallon Mercière. Here, take a secondary valley among trees and large blocks to 2200m, then turn east to the Lac de Tavels. Reach the Baisse de la Lause (2632m) to the north by gentle slopes and a steep finale. Descend west to the Lac Supr. de Valescura (2439m) and climb steep and avalanche-prone slopes west to the Baisse du Druos (2560m). Descend west to the Lacs de Terre Rouge and then south-west to Isola 2000.

Some steep energetic skiing.

5a (two days)   This goes north from the Col de Salese and passes to the Italian side of the frontier and is committing. The route links Brèche Margiole, Rif. Questa, Col de Valescura, Passo d'Orgials, St. Anna di Vinadio, Passo Tesina, Callieri and St. Bernolfo. This requires two ten-hour days of skiing with either a bivouac or a night at Rif. Questa (locked – key at Coni). An escape to the north by the main valley is avalanche-ridden and that to the south steep. However, with good weather a competent party will succeed with bivouacs before traversing the Corborant to Rabuons Section (see Section B and Bibliography).

Magnificent!

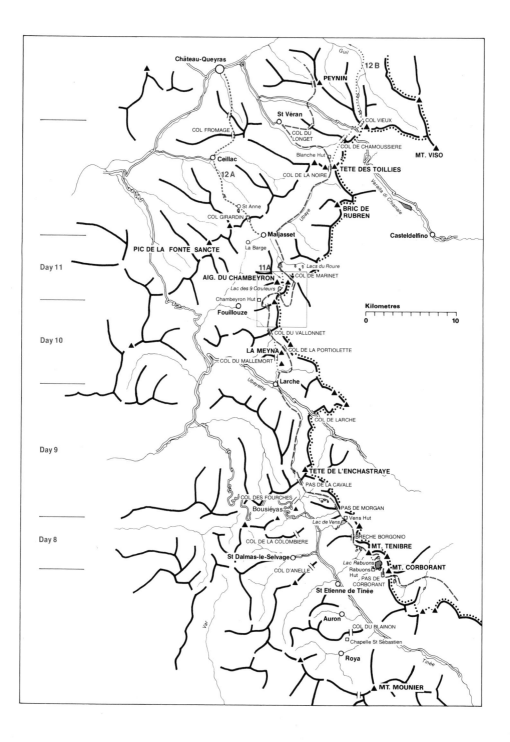

The Winter Traverse (pictures 1 to 17)   1   The view east from Cime W de Fenestre to Pas du Mt. Colomb
with Mt. Ponset to its right and Grand Mt. Capelet beyond (Day 4)

2   The authors at the Nice Hut after their Mt. Clapier descent (Day 2)

3   *Approaching the Rabuons Hut (Day 7)*

5   *Mt. Ténibre from Auron. The route traverses the range from right to left (Day*

The view south-east to Maritime Alps from Pas de Corborant (Day 7)

6   *The Rabuons Hut and the Tête des Chalanches (Day 7)*

7   *Col de la Portiolette and La Meynat from Col du Vallonet (Day 10)*

8 (top left) At the Col de la Noire with the Ubaye Valley and the Chambeyron massif in the background (Day 12)   9 (right) Ascending the Torrent du Vallon Cros (Day 14)   10 (lower left) In the Nevanche Valley (Day 16)

12   *On the Pas du Lac Blanc – looking south (Day 16)*

13   *The Polset-Peclet group from Col du Labby (Day 19)*   14   *Grande Cass*

15   *The ascent to Col de la Croix Fretes (Day 20)*   16   *(lower right) Col du Lac Noir and the Ruit*

Grande Motte, the highest peaks in the Western Graians, seen from Col du Dard (Day 19)

area seen from the Col above the Argentière Glacier –   Mt. Blanc in the distance (Variant 22a)

17   Above Samoëns
(Day 28)

18   (below) Dents d'Odda
from beneath the Col de
la Golèse (Day 28)

THE TRAVERSE OF THE SOUTHERN ALPS
(Isola 2000 – Briançon)

This traverse, particularly the section between Isola and St. Véran is, in spite of the limited altitudes and the absence of glaciers, among the finest and most demanding in the Alps because of its extremely isolated atmosphere, steep final slopes and difficult route finding. The itinerary described is probably the best and most feasible, but for parties that wish to change it, variants are included. (Cross references to these are given in the text.) Bivouac equipment is essential.

Route Summary

Isola – Col de la Lombarde – Passo Tesina – St. Bernolfo – Pas de Corborant – Mt. Ténibre – Brèche Borgonio – Pas de Morgon – Pas de la Cavale – Larche – Col de la Portiolett – Col du Vallonet – Pas de la Couleta – Col de la Gypière – Colle dell'Infernetto – Colle di Giaslaras – Col de Marinet – Col de la Noire – Col du Longet – Pic du Fond de Peynin – Col du Vallon Cros – Les Fonds – Briançon.

Mountain Rescue

St. Sauveur sur Tinée Gendarmerie Tel. 93.02.00.07
Peleton de Gendarmerie de Haute-Montagne Briançon Tel. 92.21.10.42
Peleton de Gendarmerie de Montagne, Jausiers Tel. 92.81.07.60

Avalanche Risk Assessment and Weather Reports

St. Auban sur Durance Meteorological Office Tel. 92.64.17.33
Recorded Outlook Tel. 92.64.90.50
Briançon – Place du Eberlé Meteorological Office Tel. 92.21.07.91
Recorded Outlook Tel. 92.20.10.00

Hut Information

Hut keys may be required for the Rabuons and Vens Huts (see Days 7 and 8). *Note:* Escape from the Rabuons and Vens Huts is risky. Carry enough food to see bad weather out.

Day 6 Reach the Col de la Lombarde by chair-lift (singles are not sold), or skin up, and descend north-west to La Malgheria (1908m). Follow what can be seen of the road north-west to the St. Anna sanctuary. Continue north-west to reach the Passo Tesina (2360m). Descend steeply NW to gentler slopes and follow the Roccias Lion valley to La Capanna (1950m). Follow the Val. Tesina and reach Callieri (bivouac) via woodland. Continue south-west by the left bank of the stream up to St. Bernolfo (bivouac).

There are few such isolated spots once Isola 2000 is forgotten.

Day 6a From Isola 2000 descend the road (Val. de Chastillon) to the bottom of the Val. de la Guerche. Follow this to the Col de la Guerche (bivouac at junction with Val. du Lausfer). Descend nor-

Only less good than Day 6 because of the road section.

nor-west to the Lago di St. Bernolfo. Follow the track through ruins past CAI hut Del Laus, and continue in thick woodland to St. Bernolfo. Escape is possible further into Italy if necessary, via Bagni di Vinadio (small ski resort) and Pianche – no public transport.

The Del Laus hut is closed in winter.

Day 7 Follow the Val. di St. Bernolfo south-west by the left bank and around 1950m go obliquely west in a curving valley. Around 2200m head north-west, cross the stream and reach the lower Lansfero lake (2501m). Continue to the upper lake and contour it to the east and the dominating spur to the left (west). The Pas de Corborant (2925m) is visible immediately to the left of the summit of the same name. Sweep left (west and north) and get as high as possible before taking off the skis and reach the Pas by the steep couloir. Descend steeply north, keeping beneath the Pas des Chalanches (immediate neighbour), and then in the beautiful valley until beneath the Cime d'Ischiator. Descend steeply west and traverse above the south-east shore of the Lac Rabuons to the Rabuons Hut (82).

A long totally isolated ascent.

You may have to cut through a cornice at the Pas de Corborant and jump turn down the other side.

Day 8 Ascend Mt. Ténibre (3031m): either by going north-east up to Lac Chaffour, north-west to Lac de le Montagnette and the Pas de Rabuons and then west to the summit; or by following the large cwm north-west of the hut, which is followed by the steep south couloir and a delicate ridge traverse common with the other route. The latter is shorter and steeper requiring ice-axe and crampons in hard snow conditions. The descent west then south-west from the summit is very steep (45/50°) and requires care; at around 2950m, ski more easily (or, if skis have been taken off, put them back on) and follow a vast couloir west towards the Lacs Varicles. Do not lose height once beneath the step (between 2650m and 2600m) but traverse north then north-west to the eastern Lac de Ténibre (2583m). Cross it and head north-west then north in a vast cwm to the Brèche Borgoni (2904m) – steep finale, best taken on the left. Descend north then north-west to join the Lac de la Montagnette and continue nor-nor-west by gentle slopes to the Lacs de Vens. The Vens Hut (110) is situated on a small promontary between the valley and the upper lake.

A harsh and exciting day.

Day 9 Reach the Collet de Tortisse (2591m) north-west of the hut by following the line of the summer path, and traverse north to the Col de Fer (2584m). (A descent north-east to Ferrière and Bersezio is possible.) An ascending traverse north-west leads to the Pas de Morgon (2714m). Descend gentle slopes north-west then west to Pointe 2183m (escape possible to the south-west to the Col des Fourches and Bousiéyas (22)) and strike north to the Lac d'Agnel.

Easier going.

Climb steeply to the north-west to the Pas de la Cavale (2671m). The Pas de la Cavale is avoidable via Bousiéyas, Col de Pelouse and the Col de la Tête Caree. Descend to the north-west to the Lac de Derriere la Croix, then contour La Croix to the west. Continue due north to the Lac du Lauzanier and Pointe 2204m, from where a descent north-east to Pointe 1985m and the long Val. Flourane leads to the Ubayette valley and Larche (1670m) (50).

The slopes leading to the Pas de la Cavale are avalanche prone and should be treated accordingly.

Civilisation at last!

Day 10 Follow the Vallon Rouchouze north-east then east to the junction with the Viraysse valley and follow the latter north-west. At around 2600m in the bottom of the valley go obliquely left, and climb a steep couloir to reach the Col de la Portiolette (2692m).

Descend steep slopes to the north-west and at around 2560m traverse to above the Lac du Vallonet Inf. (This is more easily accessible via the Col de Mallemort to the south.) Continue north to the Col du Vallonet and the Lac Sup. Contour the Tête de Plate Lombarde (*42*), then traverse nor-nor-west and upwards to reach the Vallon des Aoupets, which is easily followed to the Pas de la Couleta (2750m). Descend west-nor-west and keep over to the left before skiing to the Lac Premier and the Chambeyron Hut (28). The descent west to Fouillouze is delicate. The Pas de la Souvagea (2889m) is easily reached and a difficult descent north-west provides access to the Ubaye valley.

Gives you an idea of what to expect.

Day 11 From the hut go east to the Lac Long and into the Chambeyron cirque to the Croix Bujon until a small depression (around 2800m). Go east towards the Lac des Neuf Couleurs (Variant 11a), leave it on the left and climb gently east-south-east to the Col de la Gypière (2927m). Descend to the south down the Vallon de Stroppia to the lake (2809m) (*101*). Go obliquely left (slight ascent) to reach a small col and the Barenghi bivouac hut (10). Traverse, in order to cross by a second col (2750m), the spur descending from the Brec de l'Homme's (3211m) south ridge. A short ascent followed by a horizontal traverse north-east beneath the east slopes of the spur (and above the Lago della Finestra) lead to a third small col around 2820m; another horizontal traverse north-east leads to the Colle dell'Infernetto (2783m – steep slopes). Descend north-west by the right-hand couloir (very steep) for 100m, then cross the plateau (2700m) that dominates the Infernetto valley to the north. A steep ascent to the north leads to the shoulder of Monte Ciaslaras, and at around 2950m take the less steep slopes further west to the Colle di Ciaslaras. Descend steeply to the north-east down the left-hand couloir for 100m and skin gently up to the Col de Marinet (2784m) – or reach the Col de Mary (2641m) by an easterly traverse after the descent, and follow the Vallon de Mary to Maljasset. Descend to the north-west (keep to the right) and reach the east Lac de Marinet (2532m). Pass by the ruins of the Marinet bivouac hut, then go west of a boss, and descend steeply and delicately north-east, then east and finally south-east into the Vallon de Mary at a barn at 2293m. Follow the mule track to Pointe 1912m. Cross the Ubaye river and follow the road past the chapel south-west to the CAF hut at Maljasset (55).

A difficult but very fine day.

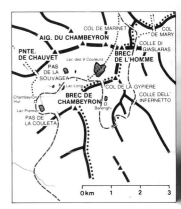

Day 11a From the Lac des Neuf Couleurs head north-east to the Col de Chambeyron (3100m) situated between the Brec de l'Homme and Pointe 3234m on the Aig. de Chambeyron. Reach it on foot by a very steep couloir; the descent onto the Marinet glacier is also very steep. Continue to the north and join the itinerary described from the Col de Marinet.

This variant requires stable snow and possibly a rope.

Day 12 From Maljasset (Variant 12a) follow the road and then the track to the bridge where the Ravin de Chabrière meets the Ravin de la Salcette. Follow the latter north-east (avalanche country); it widens after Pointe 2172m and at around 2310m ascend more steeply on the right bank of the stream to avoid a gorge. Above Pointe 2438m the valley splits. To the north the Pas de la Cula (3120m) can be taken to descend to St. Veran but this magnificent descent is exposed to avalanches and stonefall once the sun is up.

Easier going – fine skinning country.

Continue therefore north-east then east to above the Cabane du Col, which may be visible. Find the steep start for the Col de la Noire (Variant 12b), the stream bed may not be identifiable, and skin nor-nor-east to the lake and hence the Col (2955m). Descend nor-nor-east, steeply at first, and a steep slope north of Pointe 2750m leads to the Lac de la Blanche (16). From there the Chapelle de Clausis is easily reached, as is St. Véran (96) by heading west then north-west along *ski de fond* tracks in a delightfully wooded valley.

Day 12a   From Maljasset the GR5 can be followed to Briançon (112).

Day 12b   From the Col de la Noire the Agnel hut (3) can be reached via the Col de Chamoussière. Then take the Col Vieux in order to descend north to La Monta (59) and eventually Abriès (1). Reach Les Fonds (40) via the Col du Malrif (avalanche terrain).

Day 13   Go east-south-east to the Col du Longet (2701m) – compass useful – across ski-runs, through woodland and over open ground. Avoid the crags immediately west of the Col, or go back south-east up the track and 400m before the Chapelle St. Elisabeth head north-east to the col. Descend easily and enjoyably north-west, then north, then west-nor-west to the Pont de l'Ariane (2040m) (Variant 13a). Skin north then north-east parallel to the Riou des Rousses, cross the stream around 2500m, and continue north-east up large and steep slopes to the Pic de Fond de Peynin (2912m). More steep slopes lead down north-west to a barn at 2305m. Keep away from the gorges of the Peynin by following the left (south) bank steeply then less so to around 1800m. Cross the stream bed and continue north-west to reach the pistes of Aiguilles (4).

Day 13a   The slopes to the north of Pont de l'Ariane are avalanche-prone so if necessary avoid this section by following tracks to Fontgillarde, Pierre Grosse (73) and Molines-en-Queyras and then the *ski de fond* tracks to Prats Hauts. Descend steeply to Prats Bas and continue in thick forest starting in a north-westerly direction and veering gradually round to the east to the bottom of the pistes at Aiguilles (4).

Day 14   From Aiguilles walk east along the road heading for La Pause (north); it is best to follow the hairpins laboriously but steadily and put the skis on when the snow is encountered. Follow the track north-west to the uninhabited Le Lombard. Above the hamlet the valleys branch, take the left one heading west, then south-west, first up steep wooded slopes and then up gentler open ground. Continue north, following the Torrent du Vallon Cros to the col at the head of the valley (2770m). Descend north-west, avoiding a crag by moving west at around 2600m, and then follow the left bank of the stream north-west past Pointe 2313m. Return north, then north-east, past Pointe 2165m to Les Fonds (2040m) (40). Descend the road north-west (D89) to the bridge at 1859m (Variant 14a) and keep left above the stream and ski into Cervières (26). Reach Briançon by road – no public transport (23).

Day 14a   From the bridge at Pointe 1859m go north to the Cabane de Douaniers and descend north to Montgenèvre (60) on pistes. From here reach Plampinet (75) via the Col des Trois Frères Mineurs and hence Névache.

Col Girardin is very steep to the south – wind slabs sometimes to the north. The authors found it necessary to remove skis and crampon up avalanche debris on the road above Brunissard!

Great care is necessary, beneath Lac Egourgeou, after having left the trees – steep, avalanche swept slopes.

A pleasant day.

An interesting introduction to the Queyras vernacular architecture!

Typical Queyras territory.

A good way of avoiding Briançon if desired.

THE BRIANCON TO MONT BLANC TRAVERSE
(Briançon – Chamonix)

This section of the Alpine Traverse is unsustained because of the huge Arc and Isere valleys that split the massifs. This can be advantageous as sacs will be lighter and, in an area where the weather is less stable than that found further south, shelter is more easily found. The Briançon to Modane sector provides a more friendly atmosphere than the Ubaye and is less frequented and accessible than the Queyras. The views of the Dauphiné peaks are superb, the Névache valley beautiful, bivouac barns numerous, the slopes steep and the downhill skiing and route finding of particular interest. The Modane to Tignes section is grandiose and at high altitude (the Vanoise snowfield reaches 3570m); unfortunately further north, huge ski resorts (La Plagne and Les Arcs) have spoilt these mountains in places and the ski access to Bourg St. Maurice is impossible without being swamped by the hordes. This is a pity as the Bellecôte area lends itself to the ski-mountaineer, so the traverse goes illogically eastwards to the Tarentaise which, although contrived, is particularly fine. Northwards, the Beaufortain massif provides an interesting and enjoyable access to the Chamonix valley.

Route Summary
Le Tronchet – Col de Cristol – Crête de l'Echaillon – Fontcouverte – Pas du Lac Blanc – Col du Vallon – Pont de la Fonderie – Col de la Vallée Etroite – Modane – Aussois – Dent Parrachée hut – Col de Labby – Dôme des Nants – Col de Chasseforêt – Col du Pelve – Col du Dard – Col de la Vanoise – Col de la Grande Casse – Col de la Croix des Fretes – Col du Palet – Tignes – Les Pinettes – Le Fenil – Col above Glacier d'Argentière – La Motte – Bourg St. Maurice – Fort de la Platte – Col de la Nova – Presset hut – Col du Grand Fond – Col de la Croix du Bonhomme – Col du Bonhomme – Les Contamines – Col de Voza – Le Houches – Chamonix.

Mountain Rescue
Peleton de Gendarmerie de Haute Montagne Briançon Tel. 92.21.10.42
Peleton de Gendarmerie de Haute Montagne Chamonix Tel. 50.53.16.89 Tel. 50.53.16.21
Peleton de Gendarmerie de Montagne, Bourg St. Maurice Tel. 79.07.05.07

Avalanche Risk Assessment and Weather Reports
Briançon Place du Eberle Meteorological Office Tel. 92.21.07.91
Recorded Outlook Tel. 92.20.10.00
Grenoble St. Martin d'Heres, University Campus, Meteorological Office Tel. 76.54.29.63
Recorded Outlook Tel. 76.51.11.11
Recorded snow and weather report Tel. 76.51.19.29
Bourg St. Maurice Meteorological Office Tel. 79.07.04.36
Outlook Tel. 79.07.06.26
Recorded snow and weather reports (15 Dec to 30 April) Tel. 79.07.08.24

Day 15   From Briançon reach Chantemerle by road, 5.6km, and head north to Le Tronchet. Follow the road north-west to Pointe 2170m (Torrent de la Salle) and reach the Col de Cristol to the nor-nor-east (2483m). An ascending traverse to the north-west, avoiding crags at the beginning, leads to a col at Pointe 2546m on the Crête de l'Echaillon. Descend to the Torrent de Buffère, continue north around Pointe 2143m and reach the Chalets de Buffère. Follow the path (break in woodland) steeply to the valley and buildings, then ascend slightly to the road – Névache is 2.4km to the east (*66*).

Excellent descent from Crête de l'Echaillon.

Day 16   Go west-nor-west following the road for 4km to the bridge at Fontcouverte (43). A signpost points to the Ricou hut (83); follow the path steeply north to the hut. Continue behind the hut and zig-zag steeply up to the north-east, round a wide spur and up to Lac Laramon, then continue east-nor-east round another spur to the Lac du Serpent. Follow the Ravin des Gardioles until two small lakes appear. The Pas du Lac Blanc is right (south-east) of the obvious summit to the north-east; reach a small plateau to the east and go steeply north-east to it. A very steep descent leads east (jump turns) and then Pointe 2472m is more easily reached. Skin north to the Col du Vallon (2667m). Descend north by the obvious valley to the cross (east of Pointe 2197m). Turn south-east to contour the Roche Lanfol (2698m), keeping well above the right bank of the stream, and descend to the Pont de La Fonderie (1884m). Continue south-east to the Vallée Etroite hut (109), (*45*).

Astounding views and atmosphere. Make a note of the Aiguilles d'Arves – well worth a visit.

Mt. Thabor (3178m) can be done via Drayères, Col des Muandes, Col de la Chapelle du Mt. Thabor followed by a descent SE to the Pont de la Fonderie.

Day 17   Return to the Fonderie bridge and skin easily north to the Col de la Vallée Etroite (2445m) (*103*). Descend the right bank of the Combe de la Grande Montagne nor-nor-east, follow a line of buildings and descend steeply into the valley to the Lavoir chalets. Here is an Hydro-Electric Power complex. Follow the GR5 north-east through woodland to Charmaix (1574m) and follow the road to Modane, 4.8km (57).

Day 18   Cross the River Arc by the bridge in the middle of the town and walk north-east along the D215 road, turning left before Le Bourget (bivouac). Follow the wide road to Aussois (7), with a short-cut in the last hair-pin before the village. Purists will skin up the pistes from the chapel north-west to Le Vet and the Oratory to the road (note the drop!). Follow the steep ridge north-east by means of a track which leads north to the bottom of a final button lift. Here the lazy arrive from their ski-lifts (*79*), so continue north-west along the track which contours a sharp ridge and dominates the Lacs d'Amont and Aval. Cross the two streams and at Pointe 2330m head more steeply to the north-west to the Dent Parachée hut (38).

Day 18a   Modane-Col de Chavière (steep slopes just before col) via either Polset or the Orgère hut – Pralognon-la-Vanoise via the Peclet-Polset valley. Button lift to the Glière – Lac des Vaches – Col de la Vanoise.

This is not really a bad weather alternative.

Day 18b   Modane – Termignon (on public transport, therefore unsatisfactory) – Plan du Lac Hut (78) – Pont du Croé Vie – Col de la Vanoise. Or with possible continuation to Tignes via the Col de la Leisse.

The slopes in the Pont de Croé Vie area are very steep.

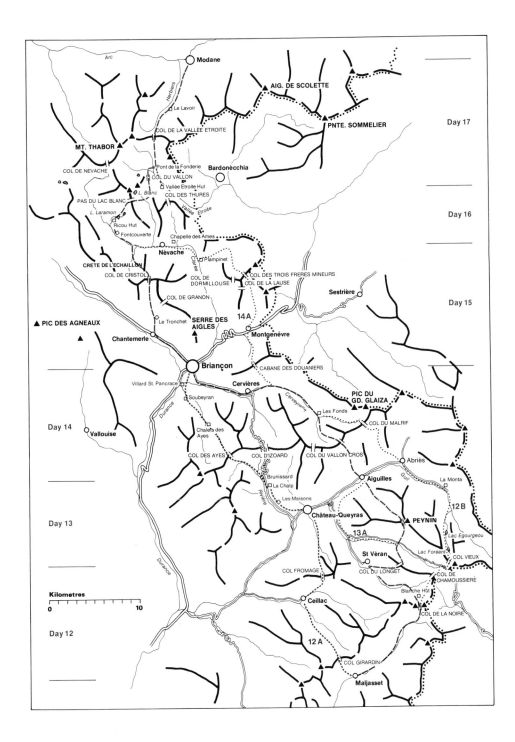

Day 19   Leave the hut early so as to reach the Col de Labby just after dawn (3328m). Go north passing Pointes 2645, 2651, 2906 and 2953m before bearing east-south-east across the Glacier du Fond; at 3220m turn north-west to the Col de Labby (3328m). Keeping height at around 3350m, traverse north-west, then north, then nor-nor-east beneath the Arête de Labby and Dômes du Génepy (crevasses and steep slopes). Contour the Dôme de l'Arpont (3599m) by the east to the Col de l'Arpont (3503m) and ascend easily the Dôme des Nants (3570m). Descend north-east to the Col de Chasseforêt (3507m) and continue north then north-east on ideal slopes to the Col du Pelve (2992m). Contour the seracs by the west side, and avoiding crevasses, curve round east then south-east up past Pointe 3958m and continue east to Col du Dard (3153m). Head north-east towards Pointe 3044m and from here enjoy the steep descent north to the Col de la Vanoise (Hut 34).

A complicated day demanding vigilance – in cloudy weather navigation is very difficult because of the absence of landmarks and presence of crevasses which would prevent parties from ski-ing on a bearing.

Day 20   Descend to Lac Long, follow its east shore and then head north steeply onto a moraine; at around 2600m strike north-east. The Grande Casse glacier is enclosed such that the only exit is the Col de la Grande Casse (3098m) to the east, which is V-shaped and easily reached. From the col descend east, then east-south-east, then north-east to a boss east of the serac-wall, which allows a passage north to Pointe 2798m. Ski steeply west, then north-west and at around 2329m the moraines force one north to the Glière chalet. Head south-west to the chapel (bivouac at Caves de la Plagne) (17) and go north-west up the obvious cwm. Once behind Pointe 2235m, follow the shallow valley (you may be unfortunate and meet off-piste skiers from Tignes here) north-east past Pointes 2336, 2388, 2471 and 2480m to the Col de la Croix des Frêtes (2643m). (Col de Palet Hut (35) close by to the north-east and descent nor-nor-west possible via Plan de la Grassaz, Plan des Eaux to Rosuel Hut (84) and Nancroix (63)). Traverse north-east to the Col du Palet (2652m) and follow pistes to Le Lac de Tignes (105) – Val Claret (107).

If you have the time and the energy, the Grande Casse (3855m) is worth doing via the Glacier des Grandes Couloirs.

Another demanding day.

Day 21   Ski down to Tignes (104), following the road if conditions allow, and follow pistes to Les Brevières. Walk north along the road to join the N202 and follow it to Les Pinettes opposite La Savinaz. Follow the road to the chapel at Chenal (1743m) and go nor-nor-east to Le Fenil (1899m) (bivouac).

A low-level day.

Day 22   Head east-nor-east through woodland well above Le Monal and continue north-east towards Pointe 2662m keeping south of the valley, soon to become a lake (when flooded as part of a Hydro-Electric Power Scheme). Reach Pointe 2662m either by the south-west slope or the south-east spur, and continue along the wide spur before traversing north-east at 2700m to reach the Lac Brulet. Cross it heading north-east keeping right (east) of the obvious crags. At about 2950m get onto the Argentière glacier and head north-west to the obvious col. Look at Mont Blanc! Descend north-west then north to Pointe 2557m and cross the corniced ridge at its best point, traverse east in between the crags and descend steeply north to Le Motte (2030m). Descend west to Le Crot (1499m) and Le Miroir south to St. Foy-Tarentaise (93). Walk or hitch to Bourg St. Maurice (21).

Superb views of Mt. Pourri (3779m) and the Dôme de la Sache (3801m).

Pointe d'Archeboc is skiable in its entirety (3272m).

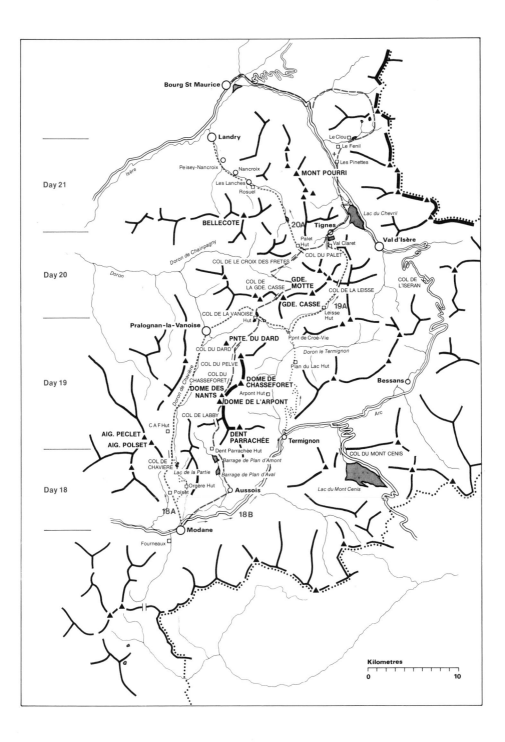

Bourg St Maurice

Landry

Peisey-Nancroix   Nancroix
Les Lanches
Rosuel

Isère

Day 21

BELLECOTE

Doron de Chainpagny

Doron

Day 20

COL DE LE CROIX DES FRETES

COL DE
LA GDE. CASSE

COL DE LA VANOISE
Hut

Pralognan-la-Vanoise

PNTE. DU DARD

COL DU DARD

COL DU PELVE

COL DU
CHASSEFORET

Day 19

DOME DES
NANTS

Arpont Hut

DOME DE L'ARPONT

COL DE LABBY

AIG. PECLET

C A F Hut

AIG. POLSET

DENT
PARRACHÉE

Dent Parrachée Hut
Barrage de Plan d'Amont

COL DE
CHAVIERE

Lac de la Partie
Barrage de Plan d'Aval

Orgère Hut
Polset

Aussois

Day 18

18 A

18 B

Modane

Fourneaux

Le Clou
Le Fenil
Les Pinettes

MONT POURRI

Lac du Chevril

20A   Tignes

Palet
Hut   Val Claret   Val d'Isère
COL DU PALET

GDE.
MOTTE

COL DE LA LEISSE

COL DE
L'ISERAN

GDE. CASSE

19A

Leisse
Hut

Ppnt de Croé-Vie

Doron le Termignon

Plan du Lac Hut

DOME DE
CHASSEFORET

Bessans

Arc

Termignon

COL DU MONT CENIS

Lac du Mont Cenis

Doron de Chaviere

Kilometres

0   10

Day 22a   An alternative route to the north takes the party into Italy and eventually to the south side of Mont Blanc via La Motte (62), Col du Lac Noir, Ruitor Hut (CAF, 88), Col du Ruitor, La Thuile and public transport to Entrèves. The Ruitor glacier section is magnificent. From Entrèves there are three possibilities and the choice will depend on the party:

From the Col du Ruitor, the summit of the Tête du Ruitor (3486) is not far away. The descent north on the glacier provides an unforgettable powder descent; but beneath the moraines the going is very steep.

(a) Follow Val Veni and reach the Gonella Hut (3072m) to join the Mont Blanc Traverse at Col du Dôme (4337m). A very difficult traverse, only suitable for the experienced.

(b) Take the Heilbronner cable car to the Aiguille du Midi and descend the Vallée Blanche, Glacier du Tacul and Mer de Glace to the Chamonix valley.

(c) Follow the Val Ferret to the Col du Petit Ferret (2488m) and descend into Switzerland to La Fouly and from there reach Verbier or Bourg St. Pierre – departure points for the Swiss High Level Routes.

The authors found this an excellent way of getting to the Dix Hut – bivouacs in a barn in the Val Ferret and at Verbier – 1st cable car to Mt. Fort.

Day 23   From Bourg, St. Maurice ski or walk north-west to Grandville and continue nor-nor-west, via Le Riontlet and Fornay, to Fort de la Platte (1993m). Leave the road at the last hairpin in order to follow a terrace north-west beneath the Deux Antoines (2401m), and continue on the right (west) bank of the Ruisseau des Vieilles. A small col (2350m) beneath the Roc de l'Enfer (2533m) allows the party to join the Vallon de Forclaz, which is climbed west, then north-west. At around 2650m turn south-west up a steep slope leading to a small summit (2840m) north-west of Pointe 2961m. Traverse its west ridge on foot until around 2800m, descend, to the north, down the right bank of a steep couloir and having passed beneath the Col de la Nova (not marked on Didier/Richard map but situated east of the Aiguille of the same name) make a descending traverse west beneath the Aiguille de la Nova (2890m). Around 2570m climb south-west to a small col found to the west of the Aiguille and from there descend south-west to the Presset Hut (81).

The Presset Hut can be reached from the south via the Ormette valley.

Day 24   From the hut climb north-east to the Col du Grand Fond (2676m). Descend the Combe de la Neuva (north-east), keeping right of a rocky boss around 2000m, and left of another, in order to join the Roselend road among fine scenery (77). Climb up north then north-east from Le Gollet and head north-east, quickly cutting across the slopes beneath the Crête des Gittes, to the Col de la Croix de Bonhomme (2443m) (Hut, 36), (31). Make a descending traverse north-west to the Col du Bonhomme (2329m). Descend north then north-east to beneath Pointe 2043m, then north-west and north-east beneath steep slopes to the Chalet Hôtel de la Balme (1706m) (9). Follow the Bon Nant valley north down gentle slopes to the Nant Borrant Hut (1391m) (64) and past Notre Dame de la Gorge to Les Contamines (36).

The traverse from the Col de la Croix de Bonhomme to the Col du Bonhomme needs stable snow.

Day 24a   For the highly experienced – a very diff'cult traverse is possible from the Col du Bonhomme to the Refuge d'Argentière, via the Col des Tufs, Col de la Seigne, lac de Miage, Ref. Gonella (CAI), Col des Aigs Grises, Piton des Italiens, Mont Blanc, Col de la Brenva, Mt. Maudit, Col du Midi, Ref. du Requin and the Col des Gds. Montets. This would enable the party either to continue eastwards via the Swiss High Level Route or to join the Chamonix valley at Argentière. (See Bibliography).

It's only been done a few times.

Day 25   Continue along the valley floor north and ascend the Col de Voza (1653m) via La Villette, Le Champel and Bionnassay (14). From the Col de Voza (13), descend pistes (green one recommended) to Les Houches (44), (*102*) and then walk or take a bus to Chamonix (29).

An easy day.

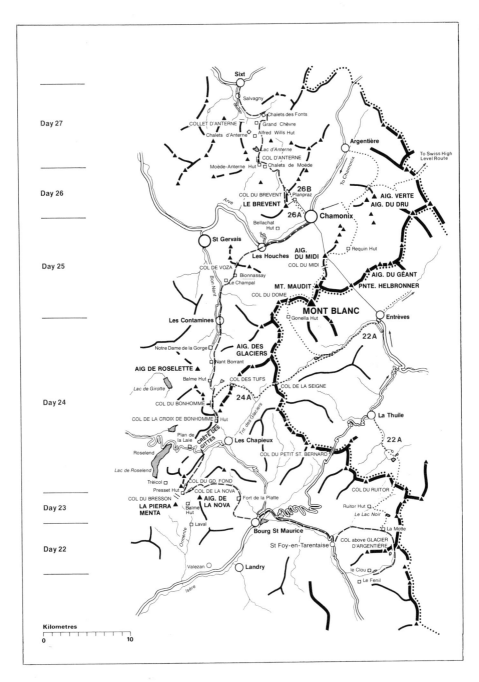

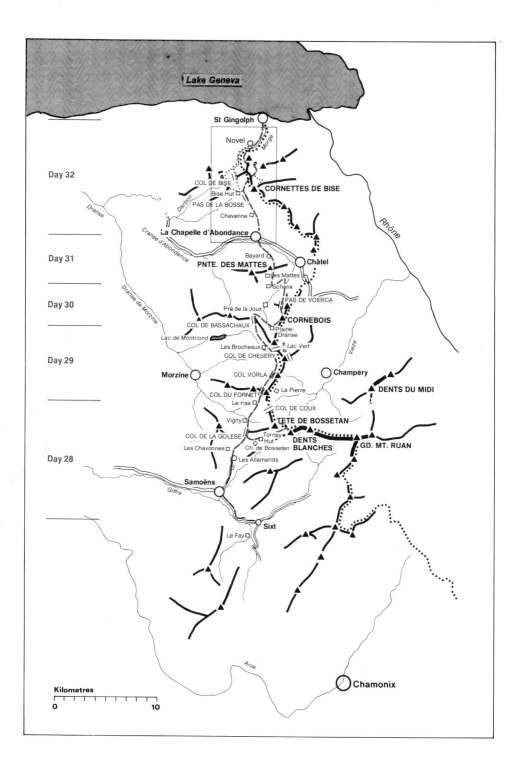

Lake Geneva

St Gingolph

Novel

Morge

Day 32

COL DE BISE
Bise Hut
PAS DE LA BOSSE
Chevenne

Dranse

Darbon

CORNETTES DE BISE

Rhône

La Chapelle d'Abondance

Dranse d'Abondance

Day 31

Bayard
PNTE. DES MATTES
Les Mattes
Schenk

Châtel

PAS DE VOERCA

Day 30

Pré de la Joux

CORNEBOIS

Dranse de Morzine

COL DE BASSACHAUX
Lac de Montriond

Plaine-
Dranse

Les Brocheaux
COL DE CHESERY

Lac Vert

Vieze

Day 29

Morzine

COL VORLA

Champéry

COL DU FORNET
Le Pas

La Pierre

DENTS DU MIDI

COL DE COUX

Vigny

COL DE LA GOLESE
Les Chavonnes

Tornay
Hut
Ch. de Bossetan

TETE DE BOSSETAN

DENTS
BLANCHES

GD. MT. RUAN

Day 28

Les Allamands

Samoëns

Giffre

Sixt

Le Fay

Arve

Chamonix

Kilometres
0   10

THE HAUTE SAVOIE HIGH LEVEL ROUTE
(Chamonix – St. Gingolph)

The Chamonix valley is linked to Lake Geneva by traversing the Aiguilles Rouges, Faucigny and Chablais massifs. From the Aiguilles Rouges and Faucigny, the views of the Mt. Blanc range are unsurpassed and the little-known Dents de Midi range under its winter snow impressively dominates Chablais. The route is best done in mid-winter because escape is easy in case of bad weather and because there is plenty of powder snow in spite of the modest altitudes. The itinerary keeps its distance from the frontier ridge in order to avoid, as much as possible, the vast piste networks found in the area, and bivouackers will appreciate the lack of huts and choice of barns.

Route Summary
Le Brévent – Col du Brévent – Col d'Anterne – Grasse Chevre – Sixt – Samoëns – Col de la Golèse – Col du Fornet – Col Vorla – Col de Bassachaux – Cornebois – Pnte des Mattes – La Chapelle d'Abondance – Pas de la Bosse – Col Floray, Col de Bise or Col d'Ugeon-Novel – St. Gingolph.

Mountain Rescue
Peleton de Gendarmerie de Haute – Montagne, Chamonix Tel. 50.53.16.89 and 50.53.16.21

Avalanche Risk Assessment and Weather Reports
Lyon Bron Meteorological Office Tel. 7.826.73.74
Maison de la Montagne, Chamonix Meteorological Office Tel. 50.53.21.41
Outlook Tel. 50.53.03.40
Recorded snow and weather report Tel. 50.53.17.11

Day 26 Unfortunately the Brévent summit is best reached by the Brévent cable-car from Chamonix via Planpraz (Variants 26a and 26b).   *No question of relaxing!*
    The Col de Brévent is not crossed but a point beneath it is reached by following the piste north from the summit and when it crosses a ridge to the east a traverse north-east must be made.
    Descend steeply to the north-west, keeping left of a point (2304m), to gentler slopes around 2200m. A descending traverse to the north-west to around 2000m then north beneath the Chalet d'Arlevé ruins (1870m), enables one to join a forest-path (through alder bushes, on avalanche-prone slopes), which is followed to the Pont d'Arlevé (1597m). This descent can prove problematical if great care is not taken in route finding. From the bridge make an ascending traverse to a small col (1685m) north of the Tête de Jeubont. Continue more or less horizontally to join the valley bottom and follow it to the Chalets de Moëde (1878m) – bivouac.
Day 26a From Chamonix reach Planpraz by following the forest-path or by following the piste (3 hrs).

Day 26b From Planpraz (1999m) go towards the hotel, then go west up the lower part of the Brévent piste until a little beyond the spur of the Pointes des Vioz, which the piste crosses by a narrow cutting. Go nor-nor-west to the Col du Brévent (2368m) by a steep couloir.

Day 27 From the chalets, go north-west easily to the Moëde-Anterne Hut (58) (1996m) and then go towards the Col d'Anterne (2264m), passing between the huge crag beneath the left ridge of column-like appearance and a smaller one immediately above the hut – a steep finalè. (From here the Tête de Moëde and Frête de Moëde and Villy provide excellent viewpoints.) Descend north to the Lac d'Anterne, then bear north-east (5), remaining between 2100m and 2200m, before continuing north-west to the Bas du Col d'Anterne (2046m). The descent to the north is delicate: do not be tempted by the inviting slopes and couloirs to the right and left. Follow the ridge on its left until beneath the pylons and follow these to the north-west to Grasse Chèvre (1694m). Do not go left via Joux Basse but head east following the summer-path in forest to the Pont des Mitaines (1400m) in the Chaux ravine and then north to the Chalets des Fonts (41). Go west along the track, care required for the Ravin des Fonts (1274m), to Salvagny. Continue along the road to Sixt (99).

Escape via Servoz – south-west – is valid. It seems better to follow the line of the summer jeep track.

Day 28 From Sixt follow the road to Samoëns (1 hr) (98). Go to Les Moulins and follow the road nor-nor-east to Les Allamands. Cut north-west up a nice slope to the road at 1198m, continue up the ridge north-east to 1380m and head for the Chalets de la Croix. Remain above the valley bottom and continue north-east to the wide Col de la Golese (1684m). To the south-east the Tornay (or Bossetan) Hut (106) is easily accessible, and the subsequent ascent of Tête de Bossetan is well worthwhile. Descend nor-nor-east to Vigny (1461m) (111) and zig-zag down in forest to the cross-country tracks in the valley (49), (61). Signposts help to reach Le Pas by a track to the north (70).

Low level enjoyment, nice views of the Dents du Midi.

Day 29 Go east-nor-east to Le Beau Bornon and head north-east in the large cwm to the Chalets de l'Aiguille (not visible). Cross the ridge behind the chalets to the north and reach the Col du Fornet (2218m) to the north-east. The huge piste networks of Avoriaz are unavoidable, so traverse pistes north-east to the Col Vorla and descend the fine piste behind to Les Brocheaux (Bar) – bivouac at Le Lindaret (north-west). From Les Brocheaux, an ascending traverse north-west leads to the Col de Bassachaux (1783m), which overlooks the Montriond lake. Follow the road east then south-east to the Chalets de Plaine Dranse (74).

Fine views from Col de Bassachaux.

Day 30 Head south-east then north-east in the large cwm (chair-lift) and reach the summit of Cornebois (2204m). Descend north-west then north-east on enjoyable slopes (sometimes easily between crags) to above the Chalets d'en Haut. From the foot of the crags of the north-west ridge of Pointe 2233m, ascend the cwm to the east up to the track which traverses north at the head of the cwm and follow its line to the Pas de Voerca. Descend the black piste north to the valley (38) and follow the road south-west to Très les Pierres (little known, ask for the chapel). Très les Pierres may be reached directly by descending the valley from Plaine Dranse. From behind the chapel, follow the extraordinary forest-path west to Ertre, and then head north to Schenk (bivouac).

Day 31 From Schenk go nor-nor-east, past Les Mattes, to the Pointe des Mattes (2009m). Descend north-east to the Chalets de la Torrens and continue to around 1600m. Contour to the north-west into the valley (Rau. des Mattes) and, keeping well away from the slopes to the west, descend north to the road, which is followed north then north-west. Descend north-east into the valley by a gap in the trees and reach La Chapelle d'Abondance (30). La Chapelle may be reached directly from Très les Pierres by following the valley bottom.

Day 32 Follow the road north to the Chalets de Chevenne (1250m). A short steep section in woodland to the nor-nor-west leads to more open ground dominated by the Cornettes de Bise. Continue past the Chalets de la Cheneau to the Pas de la Bosse (1820m) (Variant 32A). Descend north-west in the valley bottom to the Bise hut (15) – avalanche country. Three valid possibilities exist for continuing; each requires stable snow:

(a) From the hut go north-east up enjoyable slopes to the Col d'Ugeon (2010m) (Variant 32B), then descend east to the Pas de Lovenex. Descend steeply to the north-west then north to Lovenex, west of the lake, and ascend the obvious col to the west. Descend slopes exposed to avalanches and join the Ravin des Nez.

(b) From the hut follow the valley to the north (then north-west) and at about 1700m go west, south-west, then north-west to Col Floray (steep). Descend steeply to the north-west and follow the east shore of the Lac de Darbon north before continuing east to the Col de Planchamp (1943m). Descend east-nor-east to the Chalets de Neuteu, and continue down the GR5 itinerary north if it can be found. It is possible, but very steep, to descend the stream to the east. Both finish in the Ravin des Nez.

(c) Follow alternative (b) to around 1700m, then head nor-nor-east to the Col de Bise (1916m) and descend north-east to the Neuteu Chalets. Descend as for (b) above.

From the head of the Ravin des Nez an enjoyable descent leads to the bridge at 923m below Novel (frontier) (68). The road heading north-east in Switzerland allows one to ski to near Pointe 654m if the snow permits; follow paths north to St. Gingolph (94).

Day 32a Recommended after a heavy fall of snow. From the Chalets de Chevenne go west-nor-west in the Seclet valley and then north-west to the Chalets de Mens. Go north into the cwm, and obliquely north-east to the col. Leaving the obvious hillock to the south, traverse east to the Pas de la Bosse.

Day 32b From the Col d'Ugeon, the ascent of the Cornettes de Bise (2432m) is highly recommended. Descend south-east to Pointe 1937m and cross the east ridge of the Tête de Lanche Naire at its foot (2050m). Traverse and ascend south-west to the summit leaving the skis just beneath. Descend by returning to Pointe 1937m and keeping nor-nor-east beneath the crag before reaching the Pas de Lovenex to the north-west.

The forest path, in the authors' experience, will require a certain degree of skill!

Alternatively, follow the GR5 itinerary which is difficult to find – dense forest and probably precious little snow, it all calls for good sense.

Unexpectedly good skiing with a characteristically Swiss arrival at St. Gingolph.

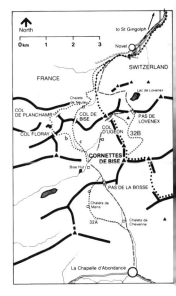

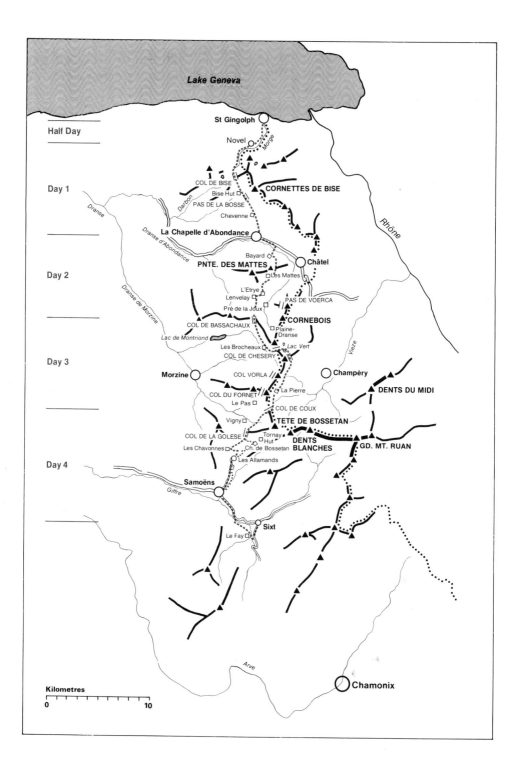

Lake Geneva

Half Day

St Gingolph

Novel

Morge

Day 1

Dranse

COL DE BISE
Bise Hut
PAS DE LA BOSSE
Chevenne

Darbon

CORNETTES DE BISE

La Chapelle d'Abondance

Dranse d'Abondance

Bayard

PNTE. DES MATTES

Châtel

Day 2

Les Mattes

L'Etrye
Lenvelay
Pré de la Joux

PAS DE VOERCA

Dranse de Morzine

COL DE BASSACHAUX

Lac de Montriond

CORNEBOIS

Plaine-
Dranse

Rhône

Les Brocheaux
COL DE CHESERY

Lac Vert

Day 3

Morzine

COL VORLA

Champéry

Vièze

La Pierre

DENTS DU MIDI

COL DU FORNET

Le Pas

COL DE COUX

Vigny

TETE DE BOSSETAN

Day 4

COL DE LA GOLESE

Tornay
Hut

DENTS
BLANCHES

GD. MT. RUAN

Les Chavonnes
Ch. de Bossetan

Les Allamands

Samoëns

Giffre

Sixt

Le Fay

Arve

Kilometres
0   10

Chamonix

THE SUMMER TRAVERSE

INTRODUCTION

The Grande Traverse in summer is best started at St. Gingolph on Lake Geneva because this avoids repeated ascents of hot south-facing slopes, and allows the route to finish near the Mediterranean coast. It can, of course, be done in the other direction. The route is divided into five sections with breaks at Sixt, Landry, Modane and Larche, and either finishing at Sospel or St. Dalmas de Tende.

Starting at the northern end the route provides enjoyable varied walking through low-level forests and alpine pastures. It then passes through Switzerland and eventually, after sustained effort, the Mont Blanc massif is revealed; and remains as a presence for a considerable number of days. The high mountain atmosphere continues as the trail continues southwards through real marmot country, the Parc National de la Vanoise, up glacial valleys and over moraines. Further on, the snowy Dauphiné peaks provide a dramatic backdrop to the walking.

Leaving the glacial massifs behind, the route leads south to wild, rocky ranges. As the route heads towards the Mediterranean the going does not get any easier, firstly over wild moor-like alpine pasture and then on barren arid shoulders. The rugged and complicated Mercantour massif is then reached with its herds of ibex and chamois and numerous lakes.

It must be remembered that in the Alps snow can linger up until late July and the only possible times of year for the walking traverse are the summer and early autumn.

For those wishing to sleep comfortably, huts and hostels (gites d'etape) are at their disposal, and others can camp where they like (except in National Parks) or partake of these comforts if they so desire.

No special techniques are required; paths are generally good and there is no scrambling involved (except for some of the additional summit ascents mentioned in the margin notes), only on late névés may parties have to use crampons or cut steps. What the traverse does require is a love of the mountains in all their forms, as much mountain experience as possible and a good pair of legs.

Route Finding
This is made easy by the presence of frequent horizontal red and white paint marks on trees, boulders and walls, which are doubled when the route changes direction. Signposts marked GR5 (with destinations, their facilities and distances in time) are numerous. An over-reliance on waymarks, however, is inadvisable, as in places they are misleading. When in doubt consult the map.

Equipment
Take the same precautions as should be taken in Britain. In addition, allow for sun-protection and water loss (avoid as much as possible drinking in streams). It is advisable to carry snake serum (available in all French chemists) in the First-Aid kit.

THE CHABLAIS AND FAUCIGNY MASSIFS
(Lake Geneva-Sixt)

This section is predominantly of a pastoral nature. A large number of agricultural dwellings compensate for the widespread evidence of the ski-economy. By alpine standards it is an unfrequented walking area, and it is complemented by views of inviting limestone summits such as the Dent d'Oche, the Cornettes de Bise and the Dents du Midi.

Route Summary
St. Gingolph – Col de Bise – Pas de la Bosse – La Chapelle d'Abondance – Les Mattes – Col de Bassachaux – Col Chesery – Col de Coux – Col de la Golese – Samoens – Sixt.

Mountain Rescue
Peleton de Gendarmerie de Haute-Montagne, Chamonix Tels. 50.53.16.89, 50.53.16.21

Weather Reports
Chamonix Tel. 50.53.03.40

From the bus-stop at St. Gingolph (94) go beneath the railway bridge and go right at a fountain/tap – first waymark. Follow the path up the wooded left bank of the stream and just beneath Novel, the path crosses the road to follow a grassy track to the village (68).

Day 1 Follow the road to the south-west out of Novel to its end, some short-cuts can be taken but don't follow waymarks which lead to La Planche. A signpost points the way across a small bridge. Follow the path sou-sou-west to the Chalets de Neuteu (1705m). Go west and an unobvious junction takes you south to the Col de Bise (1916m). Descend easily south then south-east to the Bise Hut (15). Ascend steeply east then sou-sou-east to the Pas de la Bosse, the path then descends easily to the Chalets de Chevenne. Follow the road to La Chapelle d'Abondance (30).

Hard going for a first day. Look carefully for the right way out of Novel.

Day 2 Follow the main road south-east through La Pantiaz and at a crossroads at the exit of the village (opposite Les Airelles), go south along a small road (*33*), cross the river by the bridge. Follow the road, track and then path steeply to the Chalets s/Bayard. Follow the track for about 300m south-east and then head up through dense woodland on a vague track to a clearing; with intermittent waymarks and occasional path climb steadily up to the Chalets des Grottes. Go south-west steeply to the Chalets de la Torrens and eventually Les Mattes. Join a path just above Le Pron, make a descending traverse to l'Etrye and beyond, zig-zag up south-west between the woods to the large path, follow it to Le Lenlevay and continue south on a good path to the Col de Bassachaux (1783m) (Bar Restaurant open 10 July – end of September) (*74*).

Even harder for a second day.

The D/R blue line represents a good path which the GR5 follows only at the very beginning.

For those camping at Châtel, follow the road south-west to the Pré de la Joux and go up the path (south-west, signpost) to the Col de Bassachaux.

Day 3   From the Col (*61*) an ascending traverse south-west leads to the Col de Chésery (2000m) on the French/Swiss border. Head for the obvious barn to the east-south-east and either take the large path above the north-east shore of the Lac Vert to the col to the south-east, or cut directly across on the south-west side of the lake. An obvious path descends south-east, then west, then south past various buildings (*76*); pass beneath a chair-lift and continue the traverse before descending to La Pierre and Poya. A good path to the south-west leads to the Col de Coux (1900m) (*49*). Descend to the south-west into forest, where the path has been obliterated by forestry work, from time to time waymarks appear – don't be confused by red and white forestry paint-marks. The exit from the forest corresponds with the end of a road (*70*), (*111*).

Have a good look at the unusual views of the little known alpine summits such as the Gd. Ruan etc.

Forget your Country Code in this Swiss section where electric fences often get in the way.

Day 4   Follow the path south-west easily to the Col de la Golèse (1684m spring) (*106*). From here, reach the road above Les Allamands, either via Les Chavonnes or the Chalets de Bossetan. From Les Allamands follow the road to Samoëns (98); the path marked in the forest is typical low-level forest walking and in places it is lost among cross-country ski pistes. From Samoëns follow the N507 road and at the exit of the town turn right after a bridge, follow the right bank of the Giffre until opposite Le Perret. Turn right and after the chapel follow the path scenically through the Gorges de Tines to Le Fay and Sixt (99).

The Tête de Bossetan (2406m) can be done from the Tornay Hut – some scrambling involved.

Some ladder sections in the Gorges de Tines.

SUMMER TRAVERSE : SECTION B

THE AIGUILLE ROUGES AND BEAUFORTAIN MASSIFS
(Sixt – Landry)

Mont Blanc and its satellites dominate this section. Savouring the atmosphere of this unique area, one can understand who so many British climbers have been attracted by the Mont Blanc range for so many years. The small and particularly unspoilt Beaufortain is an ideal viewpoint for things to come, and the contrast felt with the crowded Mont Blanc Tour renders the walking delightful.

Route Summary

Sixt – Chalets d'Anterne – Col d'Anterne – Col du Brévent – Le Brévent – Les Houches – Col de Voza – Les Contamines – Col du Bonhomme – Col de la Croix de Bonhomme – Crête des Gittes – Plan de la Laie – Col du Bresson – Landry.

Mountain Rescue

Peleton de Gendarmerie de Montagne, Bourg St. Maurice Tel. 79.07.05.07

Weather Reports

Bourg St. Maurice Tel. 79.07.06.33

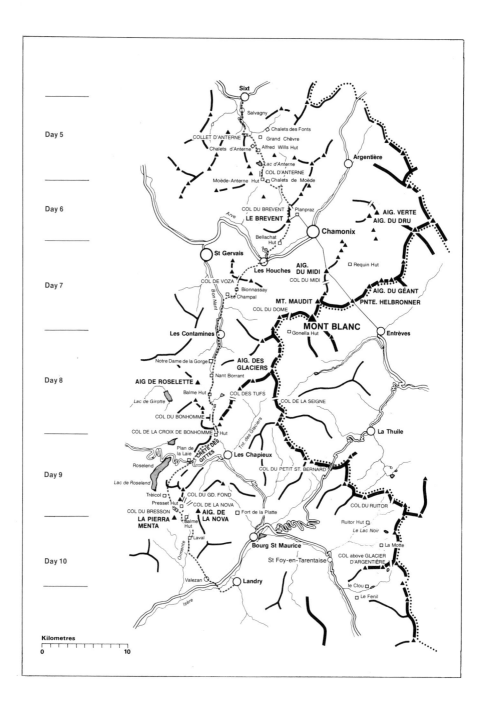

Day 5

Day 6

Day 7

Day 8

Day 9

Day 10

Kilometres

0   10

Day 5 From Sixt follow the road south, via Maison Neuve and Salvagny (*41*), to the Pont de Sales; or from Le Fay head south to the river and follow it to the Pont de Sales. The path short-cuts the road past the Chalets de Fardelay (fountain) and Lignon, and continues south-west to the Cascade de la Pleureuse. Turn left (east-nor-east) and reach the Collet d'Anterne. Descend and traverse to the Chalets d'Anterne (1807m) (*5*). The path ascends steeply south-east and winds its way south down to the Lac d'Anterne. Remain on the east shore of the lake and head south to the Col d'Anterne (2264m), a balcony offering breathtaking views of the Mont Blanc range. A steep descent south, bearing right to avoid a crag, leads to a jeep track, which is followed east to the Moëde-Anterne Hut (spring) (*58*). From here the Col du Brévent (Day 6) is easily identified by its snowy right-hand and rocky left-hand ridges.

An extraordinary variety of walking in just one day.

Day 6 Descend south-west then east to the Chalets de Moëde, and follow the path easily to the Pont d'Arlevé, from which it steadily rises south to the Col du Brévent (2368m). (From here the path down to Chamonix (*29*), (*102*) is obvious and easily followed.) From the col traverse enjoyably south-west among boulders to Le Brévent (2525m). (A descent to Chamonix can be made in the cable-car via Planpraz. From a point just north of the summit of Le Brévent a path descends north-east, via 'La Chemineé', to Planpraz.) From the summit of Le Brévent continue south-west on the Mont Blanc Tour (MBT) to the Bellachat Hut (11).

When snow covered, the slopes beneath the Col du Brévent may require great care and even the competent use of ice-axe and crampons in early morning.

Day 7 Descend steeply to the south-west to the zoo! Follow the road west to Le Coupeau, and take a short-cut south to the railway station at Les Houches (44), (*102*). Cross the bridge at the dam, go steeply up the road and pass through the town to the Bellevue cable-car station. Turn left (signpost) and follow a road and then a track to Les Trabets (bar), and continue following the obvious path and signposts to the Col de Voza (bars, 1653m). Descend the track south then south-west to Bionnassay (1314m) (14). The path drops down to the stream and rises steeply up the other side to join a large track, which is followed to Le Champel and La Villette (signposts). The MBT and GR5 make a detour here via La Gravaz and join the main road at Tresse. To avoid following the main road to Les Contamines, turn right over the bridge for Le Quy, and follow a track to Les Hoches and then a road to Nivorin (36), (*51*).

Unforgettable views if the weather is fine.

You will be meeting people doing the MBT.

Day 8 Follow the road sou-sou-west, cross the bridge at 1167m (in order to gain the right bank of the Bon Nant river) and follow a track to the bridge at Nôtre Dame de La Gorge. The track rises above the stream, crosses it by an old bridge and continues steadily, past the Nant Borrant Hut (64) and Chalet Hôtel de la Balme (9), to a plateau – beautiful scenery. At the junction for the Jovet lakes, go south-east then south-west to the Col du Bonhomme (2329m). A slight ascent, then a traverse to the south-east leads to the cairn at the Col de la Croix de Bonhomme (2443m). Descend south-east to the Col de la Croix du Bonhomme hut (37), (*31*).

The forestry work above Les Contamines was made necessary after tremendous winds up-rooted hundreds of trees.

The slope between the Col du Bonhomme and Col de la Croix de Bonhomme requires particular attention if snow covered.

Day 9 Follow the path over the Crête des Gittes (2542m) and down to the Col de la Sauce, continuing over pastures south-west to Plan de la Laie (77). Follow the track west-sou-west to La Petite Berge, and head sou-sou-west across boggy ground to join zig-zags, which lead to the ruins at 2071m. Very boggy walking and a poor path lead south-west to the Gde. Berge (in ruins). A good path leads to Dunand, and an improvised descent to Tréicol allows another good path to be followed. The path ascends in huge zig-zags to Le Presset – junction with Col de Coin. Continue south-east then east to the Col du Bresson (2469m) (81). Descend easily east-south-east into the beautiful valley beneath the magnificent Pierra Menta. Follow the path south then east in the valley to the Balme Hut (8).

When the path is covered with snow the way up to the Col du Bresson can be difficult to find – some waymarks should be visible – keep to the left.

Day 10 Descend the wide valley south on the left bank of the stream, past Laval, and at the bridge (1599m) rise slightly left. The path traverses and descends south-east, via Les Fours, to the hamlet of Valezan (108). It continues to descend due south, short-cuts the road, traverses to more short-cuts above Le Crey and descends directly to Bellentre (12). Just before reaching the church follow the road south, cross the Isere river and go along the road east to Landry (48).

Avoid doing the latter part of this descent in the heat of the day.

SUMMER TRAVERSE : SECTION C

THE VANOISE NATIONAL PARK (GRAIANS)
(Landry – Modane)

This vast and highly frequented area boasts lakes, snowy peaks, good paths on moraine or pasture, and comfortable huts. The route makes the most of all these assets. This section of the walk passes through a National Park and certain restrictions exist:
- No camping except on restricted sites   • No smoking or open fires in or near forest
- Do not pick wild flowers   • Do not leave litter

Route Summary
Landry – Nancroix – Les Lanches – Col du Palet – Lac de Tignes – Col de la Leisse – Col de la Vanoise – Pralognon – la-Vanoise – Col de Chavière – Modane.

Mountain Rescue
CRS Pralognon-La-Vanoise Tel. 79.08.71.15

Weather Reports
Bourg St. Maurice Tel. 79.07.06.26

Day 11 From Landry (rail link with Bourg St. Maurice and Chambéry) take the D87 sou-sou-east, short-cutting the hair-pin bends, and following the road pass beneath Peisey-Nancroix (72). A track leads to Le Moulin and continues to the north of the road, past some boulders to Nancroix (63). Follow the road beneath 'La Maison Savoyarde' to a track, which crosses the stream by a bridge (signpost) and then heads south-east on the left bank past the

Long but rewarding.

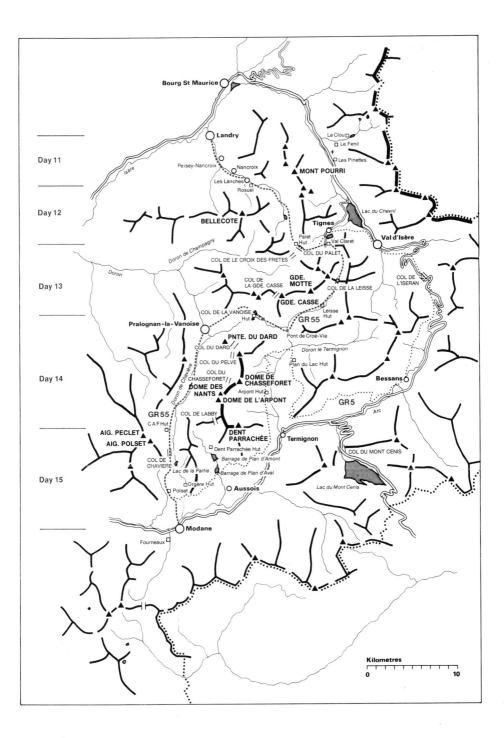

Day 11

Day 12

Day 13

Day 14

Day 15

Bourg St Maurice

Landry

Le Clou
Le Fenil
Les Pinettes

Peisey-Nancroix   Nancroix
Les Lanches
Rosuel

MONT POURRI

Isère

BELLECOTE

Lac du Chevril

Tignes
Palet
Hut   Val Claret
COL DU PALET

Val d'Isère

Doron de Chainpagny

COL DE LE CROIX DES FRETES

Doron

COL DE
LA GDE. CASSE

GDE.
MOTTE

COL DE LA LEISSE

COL DE
L'ISERAN

GDE. CASSE

COL DE LA VANOISE
Hut

GR 55

Leisse
Hut

Pralognan-la-Vanoise

PNTE. DU DARD

Pont de Croé-Vie

COL DU DARD

Doron le Termignon

COL DU PELVE

Plan du Lac Hut

COL DU
CHASSEFORET

DOME DE
CHASSEFORET

DOME DES
NANTS

Bessans

Doron de Chavière

Arpont Hut

DOME DE L'ARPONT

GR 5

GR 55

COL DE LABBY

Arc

C A F Hut

AIG. PECLET

DENT
PARRACHÉE

AIG. POLSET

Termignon

Dent Parrachée Hut

COL DU MONT CENIS

COL DE
CHAVIERE

Barrage de Plan d'Amont

Lac de la Partie

Barrage de Plan d'Aval

Orgere Hut

Lac du Mont Cenis

Polset

Aussois

Modane

Fourneaux

Kilometres

0   10

camp-sites in the forest. Continue past Les Lanches (47) to Rosuel (Hut, 84).

Day 12   The path rises east-south-east, then south-east to the Chalet de derrière la Rèbe and signposts show the way to above the Lac de la Plagne. Continue easily to the Plan de la Grassaz (periodic lake) and the Lac de Grattaleu. Go south, then south-east, then east to the Col du Palet (1652m) (Hut, 35). Descend east past ski-lifts to the Lognan chalet, and drop down to Val Claret (107).

Lots of people on this section.

A dip in the odd lake will cool you down.

Cable cars full of summer skiers can be seen on the Gde. Motte (3653m).

The GR5 now traces a huge arc via Val d'Isère, Col de l'Iseran and Termignon to Modane. The description given is the GR55 Variant, which provides better high level walking.

Day 13   From Val Claret head south-east via the Chalet de la Leisse to the junction for the Col de Fresse; head south-west among boulders and ascend the Col de la Leisse (2758m). Descend to the Lac des Nettes and a grassy track leads to the Leisse Hut (2487m) (52). Cross the stream beneath the hut and follow it west, then south-west, then south to the Pont de Croé Vie (2099m). Take the path on the right, which rises steeply west then north-west past a blockhouse, to the lakes above and the Col de la Vanoise (2517m) (Hut, 34) – grandiose surrounds.

Val Claret is for skiers – leave it to them!

Study both the Gde. Casse ordinary route which goes up the huge glacier, and the north face of the Aiguille de la Vanoise from the Lac des Vaches.

Day 14   The path continues nor-nor-west and then contours the Aiguille de la Vanoise via the Lac des Vaches (stepping-stones) to the south-west and descends past the Chalets de la Glière into forest to Les Fontanettes and eventually Pralognon-la-Vanoise (80). Leave the town via Le Barioz, cross the stream and go left along the street that leads to the tea-room 'Petit Chamois'. The path goes south-west in woodland; leave the track which crosses the Doron de Chaviere on the right at the Dabadie bridge, and follow the right bank of the river to the Pont de Gerlon. Cross this and continue along the track to Les Prioux (1711m) and follow the road on the right bank to the Pont de la Pêche. The track is easily followed south-west to beneath the Péclet-Polset Hut and then to the Col de Chavière (1796m) – excellent viewpoint and highest col on a GR path. (For those spending the night at the Péclet-Polset Hut (71), traverse south then south-east to join the main path at point 2498m).

Pralognon is a nice summer resort – try a 'fondue savoyarde' before leaving.

Day 15   Descend south among boulders and cairns to a rocky cwm and bear south-west down via Le Grand Planay and woodland parallel to, but well above, the St. Bernard stream to the hamlet of Polset (1840m, spring). (After the descent south from the Col de Chavière it is possible to descend sou-sou-east via the Orgère Hut (69) and then to follow GR5/D106 to a junction with GR55 beneath Polset – track destroyed by road-works.) To the south of Polset the mule track has been destroyed by road-works, so reach La Perrière by following the road for 50m south-east and by cutting down to the mule track, which descends in forest. Zig-zag down south-east and cross steep boulder-fields to reach Loutraz; cross the Arc to Modane (57).

A long descent to the smoky buildings of Modane.

THE THABOR, QUEYRAS AND UBAYE MASSIFS
(Modane – Larche)

Of the three massifs traversed in this section, the Queyras and Ubaye are considered to be part of the Southern Alps. The Thabor massif is very little-known, even by French mountaineers, and the walker gets an initial impression of what is to follow while still enjoying close views of the glaciers of the Dauphiné peaks. At respectable altitudes the going gets hotter, especially on southern slopes; dehydration should be guarded against and the heat of the day avoided as much as possible.

Route Summary
Modane – Col de la Vallée Etroite – Col des Thures – Névache – Col de Cristol – Col de Granon – Briançon – Col des Ayes – Brunissard – Les Maisons – Château Queyras – Col Fromage – Ceillac – Col Giradin – Fouillouze – Col du Vallonet – Col de Mallemort – Larche.

Mountain Rescue
Peleton de Gendarmerie de Haute – Montagne, Briançon Tel. 92.21.10.42
Peleton de Gendarmerie de Montagne, Jausiers Tel. 92.81.07.06

Weather Reports
Brainçon Tel. 92.20.10.00

Day 16 From Modane go to the church at Fourneaux and the d'Arrodaz chair-lift departure point. Follow the track beneath the lift, and leave it to go under a viaduct and behind one of its pillars to reach the road which leads to Charmaix. Continue up the road to a junction, bear right and go past the Chalets des Herbiers to the Chalets le Lavoir. Leave the road by a small dam, and follow the path to the Chalets la Losa and La Replanette (spring). Head for the obvious Col de la Vallée Etroite (2445m). Descend to the south, keeping right of hillock 2553m, and follow the right bank of the stream, continuing on boggy ground to the Pont de la Fonderie. From the bridge follow the road to the Vallée Etroite Hut (109), (*45*), (*103*).

Back to enjoyable pasture.

Mt. Thabor (3186m) is well worth an ascent.

Day 17 Go up steeply to the south, zig-zagging in forest past the Chavillot barns, to the lake (2194m) and the wide Col des Thures. Descend the track to the ruined Chalets des Thures, go obliquely left and descend steeply in woodland, crossing the Robion stream near an old wood-cabin, and continue south to the Chapelle des Ames (1608m) just east of the village of Névache (*66*). (Buses from Névache to Briançon Tel. 92.21.12.91)

The Col des Thures is magnificent and the Névache valley unique.

Day 18 From here GR5 goes to Briançon via Plampinet, Col de Dormillouse, Col de la Lauze and Montgenèvre. The variant GR5c is described because of its greater interest.

Take the road west to Le Cros and cross the river by a wooden bridge. The path leads south, then steeply to the west in forest and then easily to the Porte de Cristol (2483m). Follow the track south-east horizontally to the Col de Granon. After 400m on the D234 road heading south-west go left along a track to the Col de Barteaux (2382m). Take the path to the summit of the Croix de la Cime (2606m), and then follow the ridge via La Grande Peyrolle and Serre des Aigles. After l'Enrouye a forest descent leads to the Croix de Toulouse (1962m). A well-marked path on the left leads, still among trees, to Briançon (23).

Superb views of the Dauphiné Alps. (Barre des Ecrins 4102m).

Day 19   From the Porte de L'Embrun (in the old town), descend to the Parc de la Schappe, cross the Durance and follow it to the road for the Col d'Izouard. After 80m go right on a large track to Toulouzanes in order to reach the church at the Pont de Cervières. Cross the Cerveyrette stream and follow the road to Sachas. Cross the Ayes stream, leaving to the right of Soubeyran and to the left of the chapel, and go up the track in the Vallon des Ayes on the left bank of the stream to the Chalets des Ayes. Leave the road to the right, (the path, after entering the forest, was destroyed by avalanche; a new one exists) and follow the valley south-east to the Chalets de Vers le Col, and from there reach the Col des Ayes (2460m). Descend south-east towards the Chalets de l'Echaillon; before reaching them go north-east and zig-zag steeply down to easy walking south-east to Brunissard (24).

Briançon, the gateway to the Southern Alps; don't forget to visit the old town.

Day 20   From Brunissard reach La Chalp (27) by following the road (N202). From the chapel contour south-east to Les Maisons (junction with GR58, 1708m). Take the path, common to both GRs, east-south-east to the Lac de Roue and then continue east over a small plateau, descending gently then more steeply south-east to the D947 road, which is followed east to Château-Queyras (32).

A nice low-level approach to fortified Château-Queyras.

Day 21   Cross the Guil river, leaving the Sommet Bucher road to the right, and remain on the right bank of the Bramousse stream, which is crossed by the same road at 1599m. Continue on the road for 500m, leaving it to follow the valley and meeting it again for the last time near some old buildings. Do not take the obvious path next to the river, but ascend slightly to find the GR narrowly winding its way across an alp towards Pointe 2125m (road). Continue south, round the ridge, and contour easily to the Col Fromage (2301m, 100m to the east is a concrete/stone cabin for shelter if necessary). Descend south-west to Le Villard (water, ruins and junction with GR58) and go west along a track, which is left for one lower down just before arrival at Ceillac (25).

An arid day with good retrospective views.

Day 22   From the fountain in the church square, take a street left of the 'Mairie', cross the Critillan river to reach the Mélezet road and follow it for 2km. Leave the road and keep on the right bank of the stream and pass through the ski car-park. Near the Hôtel de la Cascade the path climbs south-west, after having crossed the stream by a wooden bridge right of the Cascade de la Pisse. Zig-zag steeply above Pied du Mélezet, pass a zone of heavy erosion before steeper terrain leads to the south. Go over a small bridge on the flank of a ravine to reach a stream and waterfall, along which the path rises. Once the wood has been left cross the stream and continue to the Lac des Près-Sébeyrand (2287m). From the south shore of the lake follow the path, passing near a shepherd's hut and

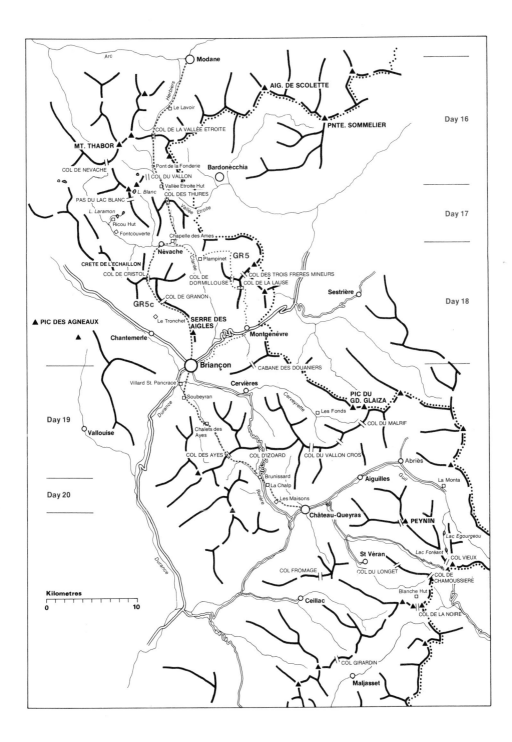

Arc

Modane

AIG. DE SCOLETTE

Day 16

Le Lavoir

COL DE LA VALLÉE ETROITE

PNTE. SOMMELIER

MT. THABOR

COL DE NEVACHE

Pont de la Fonderie

Bardonecchia

COL DU VALLON

Vallée Etroite Hut

PAS DU LAC BLANC

L. Blanc

COL DES THURES

Day 17

L. Laramon

Vallée Etroite

Ricou Hut

Fontcouverte

Chapelle des Ames

Névache

CRETE DE L'ECHAILLON

Plampinet

GR 5

COL DE CRISTOL

COL DE
DORMILLOUSE

COL DES TROIS FRERES MINEURS

COL DE LA LAUSE

Sestrière

Day 18

GR5c

COL DE GRANON

Clarée

Le Tronchet

SERRE DES
AIGLES

PIC DES AGNEAUX

Chantemerle

Montgenèvre

Briançon

CABANE DES DOUANIERS

Day 19

Villard St. Pancrace

Cervières

Soubeyran

Cerveyrette

PIC DU
GD. GLAIZA

Les Fonds

Vallouise

COL DU MALRIF

Chalets des
Ayes

Durance

COL D'IZOARD

COL DU VALLON CROS

Abriès

La Monta

Day 20

COL DES AYES

Brunissard

La Chalp

Aiguilles

Guil

Rivière

Les Maisons

PEYNIN

Château-Queyras

Lac Egourgeou

St Véran

Lac Foréant

COL VIEUX

COL FROMAGE

COL DU LONGET

COL DE
CHAMOUSSIERE

Durance

Blanche Hut

Ceillac

COL DE LA NOIRE

Kilometres

0   10

COL GIRARDIN

Maljasset

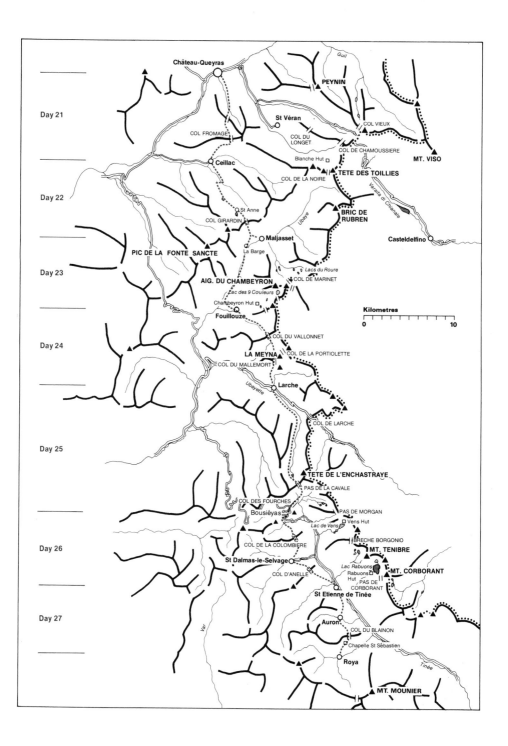

beneath a button-lift, to 100m before the upper pylon of the lift. A traverse on rocky ground leads to the Chapelle St. Anne (2415m, a pilgrimage on 26 July). Continue south-east over pasture and boulder terrain to the Col Girardin (2701m) – fine views. Descend to the south-east, zig-zagging at first and then following the stream bed, to a small hut (2470m). Continue to follow the stream to around 2380m, where a dry bed is crossed, and ascend slightly to keep above crags, then descend to the south-west into the valley 300m above La Barge (1874m). For those wishing to descend to Maljasset (hut, *55*) at around 2380m, go south-east to the cross and from there drop very steeply down a poorly-defined path.

The Ubaye is best viewed from the Col Girardin and remnants of the Chambeyron glacier can be seen.

Day 23   From La Barge descend south-west along the road past St. Antoine to the enormous block of Châtelet (1674m). Here the road splits, so take the left branch to the Pont du Châtelet (a drop of 97m to the Ubaye river) and follow more road to Fouillouze (42).

Day 24   Go south-east from Fouillouze on the right bank of the Riou, rise gradually, crossing the Riou du Vallon, and head for the col to the right of the Tête de Plate Lombarde, the Col du Vallonet (2515m). Follow, more or less, the stream from the upper lake to the lower (springs). Contour, at 2400m, the head of the Pinet valley, which is dominated by the Meyna (3065m). An old military fort is visible, and the path heads for this and the Col de Mallemort (2558m). Descend easily towards Larche; around 2100m the path disappears and progress to the east is limited by the Rouchouse stream, where a path exists leading to the village (50).

The path is a bit vague between the Col de Mallemort and Larche.

SUMMER TRAVERSE : SECTION E

THE MARITIME ALPS
(Larche – Sospel or St. Dalmas de Tende)

The Upper Tinée, with its isolated paths and ridges, flocks of sheep and stylized vernacular architecture, is a varied preface to the more abrupt Mercantour massif. The latter is a far more 'alpine' area, with some uncompromising terrain underfoot. The area is prone to afternoon storms, so early risers will make the best progress and enjoy to the full these unusual mountains.

Route Summary
Larche – Pas de la Cavale – Col des Fourches – Col de la Colombière – St. Dalmas de Selvage – Col d'Anelle – St. Etienne de Tinée – Auron – Col de Blainon – Roya – Col de Crousette – Col de Moulines – Portes de Longon – Roure – St. Saveur s/Tinée – St. Dalmas Valdeblore – Col du Barn – Col de Salèse – Le Boréon – Pas des Ladres – Pas du Mt. Colomb – Baisse du Basto – Baisse de Valmasque – Merveilles – (St. Dalmas de Tende) – Pas du Diable – Baisse Cavaline – Col de Raus – Pointe des Trois Communes – Baisse de Ventabren – Sospel.

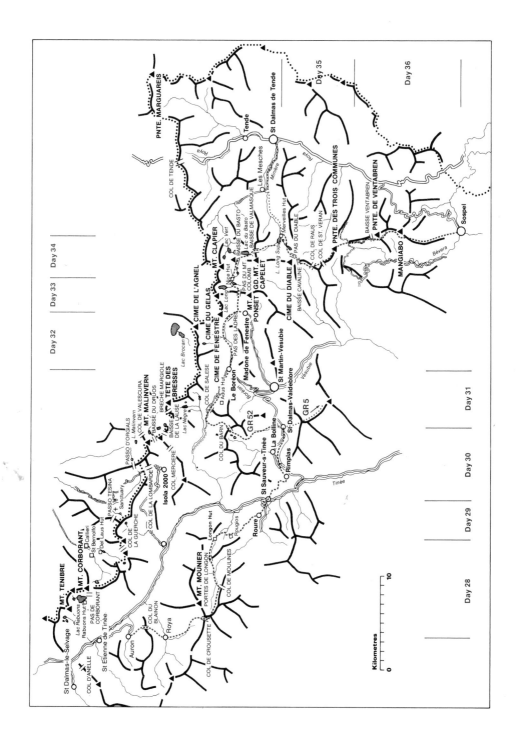

Mountain Rescue
CRS St. Martin de Vésubie (alternating with Gendarmerie Tel. 93.03.20.10
CRS St. Dalmas de Tende Tel. 93.04.60.02

Weather Reports
Nice Tel. 93.72.31.31

The following description combines the GR5 (Larche – St. Dalmas de Valdeblore) with the GR52 (St. Dalmas de Valdeblore – Sospel) because the variant provides a far better outing.

Restrictions in the Mercantour National Park are the same as those found in Section C for the Vanoise National Park except that bivouacs are allowed.

Day 25   From Larche follow the small road to the south-east past the Fouque cabin to the Pont Rouge. Follow the Flourane valley to the south-west past the Donnadieu cabin into the Vallon de Lauzanier, then continue past the chapel (2300m) to the Lac de Lauzanier. The path heads south: cross the stream, and follow its right bank to the Lac de Derrière La Croix. The path widens and the Pas de la Cavale (2671m) is easily reached. Descend steeply south-east to the Lacs d'Agnel and pass Pointe 2183m. Leave the Col du Poriac path to the left and 150m further on head west then south-west to reach the Col des Fourches (2262m), with intermittent waymarks. Descend to the south-west, short-cutting the road to Bousiéyas (22).

Care should be taken at the Pas de la Cavale, the authors were very nearly victims of falling blocks when descending SE.

Day 26   Leave the hamlet to the south-east on the D64 and in the hairpin bend take the track on the right, which crosses the Tinée river and leads to Rio-Bas. The path continues south-east and traverses a large cwm. The grassy path curves south and leads deviously to the Col de la Colombière (2237). Descend south (leave an old path to the south-east) on a path which follows the right bank of the Vallon de la Combe to St. Dalmas le Selvage (1450m) (90). Go past the church to its right and follow the dirt track south-east then south to the Col d'Anelle (1739m). Don't follow a path heading south, but take the one to the south-east, which descends easily and scenically to St. Etienne de Tinée (92).

St. Dalmas le Selvage is remarkably unsophisticated, have a look around.

The Col d'Anelle is a delight.

Day 27   Cross the bridge in front of the school and go straight on up the D39, past a petrol station, to the milestone numbered 6, where the path goes right into forest. Zig-zag past oratories to a plateau, and follow a road south into Auron (6). Follow the pylons of the Riou button lift in order to traverse the filled-in ravine, and reach a cable-car pylon. Follow the D39, cross the bridge over the Ravin des Nabines, and pass beneath the cables in front of a chalet and a fountain. Once in the forest, the path crosses the Blainon stream and leads to the Col de Blainon (2011m). Descend south-west past a barn to the St. Sébastien chapel. Traverse west and go south to La Salle and eventually to the hamlet of Roya (87).

More ski networks spoil the walking but Roya radically changes the scene.

Day 28   Descend so as to traverse the valley, and follow the right bank of the Vallon de la Maïris to the south. Pass between the Barres de Roya and rise in a south-easterly direction past a barn to beneath the Sellevielle crags. Zig-zag east and once past the crags the path leads south to the Col de Crousette (2480m). The path is easily followed to the ridge and then over vast arid shoulders south-east to the Col de Moulines (1982m). Descend steeply north-

Don't miss doing the ridge to the summit of Mt. Mounier (2817m).

west then north-east to the stream, which is crossed. A track then a grassy path lead north-east above Vignols. Cross the Gorgette valley and rise steeply among rocky scenery to the contrasting grassy valley of the Portes de Longon. The path is then easily followed east then south-east (sometimes a little vague) to the *vacherie* or Longon Hut (85).

Day 29   Continue in the same direction, a short steep section and then easier walking on a fine path lead past Rougios in forest (blueberries) to Roure (86).(Buses for St. Sauveur s/Tinée) The path cuts down very steeply crossing the road several times heading south-east to St. Sauveur s/Tinée (95).

Unusual stuff – descent all the way.

Day 30   Leave the village by the N205 and take the road for the St. Roch chapel, after the first hairpin take a good path on the right to below the chapel. Continuing up, cross a stream and traverse past La Bataille on the remarkable path to Rimplas. The path passes beneath the road and runs parallel before joining it. Follow the road for 200m and take the path on the left, which heads east to the St. Jacques chapel at La Bolline (18). Cross fields to join the N565 and the St. Joseph chapel and follow the road to St. Dalmas-Valdeblore (91). (Here the GR5 heads south.)

To make up for Day 29, an up hill day.

Day 31   Gain the obvious hairpin north of the village, and continue north in the Chanarie valley. Higher in the valley a track has been formed, but the path remains beneath it; meet a hairpin and cross the track to reach a minor col on a ridge. Continue north up grassy slopes to the Col de Veillos. Leave the track to the left and go north-east past the Lacs de Millefonts, then turn east to the Col de Barn (2452m) – fine views. Descend easily north-east then north, cross the stream in the forest so as to reach the Vacherie du Collet. Follow the track east to the Col de Salèse (2031m) (2) and continue descending to the south-east on the track, which eventually becomes a road, (a short-cut beneath the Salèse Hut (93) is useful) to above the Lac du Boréon and reach the Chalet-Refuge (19).

A hors d'oeuvre for the high mountain terrain to follow.

Day 32   Follow the road to a bridge, go left (east) to the Vacherie du Boréon (don't be confused by cross-country ski pistes), which is passed by a short-cut to the car-park. The path heads scenically north-east past the entrance to the National Park to Peyrestrèche (ruin) and a junction (signpost). Go right, first south then east, up to the Lac des Trécoulpes (2150m), and continue to the Pas des Ladres (2448m). Descend to the south to the Madone de Fenestre (hut, 54).

The imposing Cougourde (2921m) is well worth studying.
This is moufflon country.

Day 33   The path to the right of the chapel descends to the stream, which is crossed by a bridge, bear left and pass a junction with a path which goes to the south-east. Rise to the north-west up through boulders and round a shoulder beneath the Cayre de la Madone. The path leads east in the valley at the foot of the crags on the right. Continue to the small lake, from where the Pas de Mt. Colomb (really a brèche) is reached to the south-east (2548m, névé). Descend steeply south-east into the valley beneath the dam. Go left-north (waymarks crossed out) up the small path, then the track, to the lake. Follow the path which remains above the lake north, then east, then south to the Nice Hut (67). (If the lake is low and gravel banks are visible, it is quicker to follow the vague causeway to the head of the lake.)

A short day – many a chamois to be seen.

Summer Traverse
(ｐtos 19 to 30)

(right) The view from Pas de
ｏssi to the Chalets de Bisi.
 GR5 is the obvious path
ｅ distance (Day 1)

(below) The descent to the
ｔh from Col de la Golese
ｙ 4)

21   The Mont Blanc range seen from the vicinity of Col du Brevent: Aiguilles Verte and Dru (left)
the Grandes Jorasses and the Aiguille du Geant (Day 6)

22   (left) Cascade de Rouget (Day 5).   23   (right) Approaching Col du Brevent from the north (Day

24 *(above right) Pierra Menta – the fine rock peak above the Col du Bresson (Day 9)*

25 *At the Col de la Croix de Bonhommie Hut (Day 8)*

26   The approach to the Col de la Vanoise (Day 13)

27   (below) The stepping stones across Lac des Vauches (Day 14)
28   (lower left) The Ubaye massif and the Fouillouze Valley (Day 22)

30   The view v

29 (above right) Vallon de Lauzanier – where the route coincides with the GR5 (Day 25)

n the Pas du Mt. Colomb across the Madone de Fenestre valley to the Pas de Landres (Day 33)

The Mont Blanc Tour
(photos 31 to 35)

31 (top left) The view ea[...]
to Mont Blanc from
Col de La Seigne (Day 3)

32 (left) Mont Blanc an[...]
the Aig. Noire de Peutere[...]
from Val Veni (Day 3)

33 (above) The south
side of Mont Blanc seen
from below the Pas Entre[...]
Deux Saints with Col de
la Seigne (left), Col Sapin
(middle distance) with
Tête de la Tronche and
the Tête Bernardo ridge
(5a) to its right (Day 5)

34 (right) The Italian Va[...]
Ferret looking towards th[...]
Petit and Grand Ferret Co[...]
(Variant 5a)

35   The northern aspect of the Mont Blanc range from east of Col Brevent (Day 10)

Day 34   From the hut go north around a hump, descend into the small valley and cross the stream to follow the path (roche moutonée) to the Lac Nire. This is the first of four small lakes which lead east; the path remains north of them. Between the third and fourth lakes the path bears south-east and rises steeply among boulders, scree and sometimes névé to the Baisse du Basto (2693m). Descend south then south-east past a small lake on an intermittent path into the valley, where the Valmasque path is met. Ascend south-east to the Baisse de Valmasque (2549m). The descent south is steep to the Lakes in the Merveilles valley, just north of Lac Mouton go east to the Merveilles Hut (56).

Extremely rugged walking, plenty of lakes, Ibex and genepy.

Avoid the Merveilles Hut in August.

Day 35   The final section of the path keeps well away from civilisation, Sospel being the next possibility for provisions.

Head south, then west, then south-west up past the lakes to the Lacs du Diable and continue south-east to the Pas du Diable (2436m). The path leads south in this wild cwm before traversing south-west up grassy slopes to the Baisse Cavaline (2107m). Go south-west to the Col de Raus (1999m) and continue south-east via the Baisse de St. Véran (1836m), before ascending and traversing to the Pointe des Trois Communes. Grassy walking leads south-east to Plan Caval, then follow the road south past the junction below Parpella (camping, water available).

Back to grassy terrain, enjoyable airy walking.

Day 35a   A variation finish to the traverse is to descend east from the Merveilles Hut to La Minière de Vallaure and the Lac des Mesches. From there follow the road (or hitch-hike) to St. Dalmas de Tende (89).

Day 36   After 200m of road further south the path leaves the road to the right and follows an old track to the Baisse de Ventabren (1862m). Keep to the left of the Pointe de Ventabren and join the road at the Baisse de la Déa (1750m). Continue south keeping west of the Cime de la Gonella, to another small col from which leave three paths. Take the path on the right, which contours the Mangiabo, crosses a ridge (oriented west-east) and continues south into forest to a point north of the Cime Liniere. Descend the obvious ridge south to the road at the Baisse de Figuière. Cross terraces to join the road, which is followed for 400m, pass a junction, keeping straight on, and then zig-zag south steeply then more easily into Sospel (100). It is possible to catch a train from here to Nice. The GR52 continues, of course, to Menton. It is hot, sticky and dusty and is without mountaineering interest.

Well done!

THE MONT BLANC TOUR

INTRODUCTION

Mont Blanc, 4807m, is the highest summit in the Alps – the centrepiece of a crystalline massif extending 30km in length and 12 to 15km in width. Its satellite peaks, some of which exceed 4000m, are well known in alpine climbing circles, as is the French valley base, Chamonix, situated at the foot of the north side.

Its focal point as a centre for alpine climbing probably accounts for the international prestige attached to the Mont Blanc Tour, which provides the backpacker with ten days walking through France, Italy and Switzerland on varied terrain in imposing surroundings. Easy of access, relatively well frequented and well equipped with mountain huts, the Tour makes an ideal introduction for the alpine backpacking beginner. The more experienced can choose between the normal route and the more strenuous variants at higher altitudes.

Explanatory Notes

The Tour is split up into day sub-sections, which are numbered accordingly. The description is written in anti-clockwise direction around the massif: France, Italy, Switzerland, France. This is the usual direction, but it can be reversed if required. The day/number system is particularly useful for cross-referencing with variants, but also each passage represents a logical day's walking bearing in mind heavy packs and the positioning of huts, Gîtes d'Etapes and the availability of provisions. There is no point in having a day/number system for campers, who can lengthen or shorten their walking days as desired. An attempt has been made to balance the days but some are longer than others. Days 1, 2 and 3 give an idea of what is expected in terms of effort. Day 4, and to a greater extent Day 7, allow the walker to ease off a little in order to enjoy the spectacular finale.

The variants are included for those who wish to make the walking easier or more difficult.

General Information

Mention is made of local transport at the relevant point in the text. It takes the form of buses, trains, cable-cars and télécabins.

French francs are generally accepted in both Italy and Switzerland but it is better to pay in the currency of the country.

Signposting and waymarking are very good in general, but they vary from country to country. In France they are the same as for the GR5. In Italy they are generally as in France but are faded; in addition look out for red-orange triangles, circles and crosses. In Switzerland, waymarking is indicated by white-red-white horizontal stripes (sometimes outlined in black) or yellow and black in striped and diamond form.

Route Summary

Les Houches – Col de Voza – Bionnassay – Les Contamines – Notre-Dame de la Gorge – Chalet-Hôtel de la Balme – Col du Bonhomme – Col de la Croix du Bonhomme – Chalet des

Mottets – Col de la Seigne – Elizabetta Hut – Col Chécroui – Courmayeur – Col Sapin – Pas entre deux Sauts – Lavachey – Grand Col Ferret – Ferret – La Fouly – Praz de Fort – Champex – Col de la Forclaz – Col de Balme – Le Tour – Tré le Champ – La Flégère – Col du Brevent – Bellachat Hut – Les Houches.

Mountain Rescue
PGHM Chamonix Tel. 50.53.16.89   PGHM Bourg St. Maurice Tel. 79.07.05.07

Weather Reports
Chamonix Tel. 50.53.03.40   For Switzerland Tel. 162

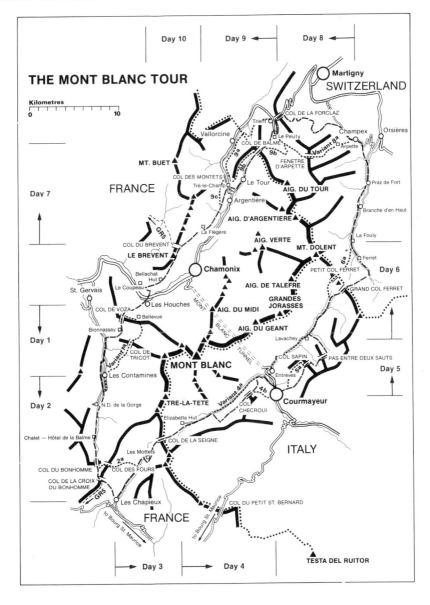

Day 1   Les Houches – Les Contamines (*For the first two days the MBT follows the same itinerary as the GR5.*)
Go left from the entrance of the SNCF station and cross the bridge at the dam, go steeply up the road and pass through the town to the Bellevue (13) cable-car station. Turn left (signpost) and follow road then track to Les Trabets (bar). Continue following the obvious path and signposts to the Col de Voza (bars, 1653m). Descend the track south then south-west to Bionnassay (1314m), (14). The path drops down to the stream and rises steeply up the other side to join a large track, which is followed to Le Champel ànd La Villette (signposts). The Mont Blanc Tour (MBT) and GR5 make a detour here via La Gravaz and join the main road at Tresse. To avoid following the main road to Les Contamines, turn right over the bridge for Le Quy and follow a track to Les Hoches and then road to Nivorin (36), (*51*).

Buses direct to Les Contamines from St. Gervais le-Fayet.

Day 1a   Les Houches – Les Contamines via the Col de Tricot (*A recommended higher level variant.*)
Follow the Day 1 route to the Col de Voza and then the tramway east to Bellevue. A good path leads east then south to the Chalets de l'Arc (1794m). Go up slightly on moraine in order to traverse the lower lip of the Bionnassay glacier, from which the Col de Tricot (2120m) is visible (look for ruined chalets). Go west across the glacier, which is flat and covered with boulders, cross a stream (which becomes swollen quickly after bad weather), pass the Chalets de Tricot and steadily ascend a large cwm to the Col de Tricot. Descend steeply sou-sou-west to the Chalets de Miage (1559m) (125) and then head west steeply up to a small plateau to the Chalets du Truc (1720m) (137). Continue down easily south-west on a track, across pasture and into forest, and then more steeply west then south-west to the car-park at La Frasse. Take a short-cut avoiding the road, past chalets, to Les Contamines.

Fine views

Day 2   Les Contamines – Les Chapieux
Follow the road heading south-west, cross the bridge at 1167m (in order to gain the right bank of the Bon Nant river) and follow a track to the bridge at Notre-Dame de la Gorge. The track rises above the stream, crosses it by an old bridge and continues steadily past the Nant Borrant Hut (64) and the Chalet-Hôtel de la Balme (9) to a plateau. At the junction for the Jovet lakes, go south-east then south-west to the Col du Bonhomme (2329m). A slight ascent then a traverse south-east leads to the cairn at the Col de la Croix du Bonhomme (2443m). Descend south-east to the Col de la Croix du Bonhomme hut (37). Leaving the GR5 to the right, descend south-east beneath the hut, past a ruined military building and the chalets at Plan Varraro, to the Chalets de la Raja (1790m, water). From here a road descends to Les Chapieux (31) – short-cuts can be followed.

Buses to Notre-Dame de la Gorge.

Beautiful scenery.

The slope between these two cols requires particular attention if snow-covered.

Day 2a   Les Contamines – Chalets des Mottets via the Col des Fours and La Ville des Glaciers (*An excellent variant which is to be recommended.*)
Follow the route for Day 2 to the Col de la Croix du Bonhomme. From the cairn go up north-east past a ruin, under electricity lines, over rocky ground and sometimes snow, to the Col des Fours (2665m). Descend east-south-east (there may be some stonefall from above) to the Plan des Fours. Follow a stream north, then

Snow often lingers in the cwm beneath the Col des Fours, where the descent between the Plan des Fours and the Chalets des Tufs can be difficult to find in bad weather.

descend north-east on steeper ground and before meeting the large stream, head east-south-east on a poor path. Cross the stream and progressively veer away from it to the left along tracks formed by animals to the Chalets des Tufs (1993m). Descend south on a good, waymarked path, being careful not to frighten the herds, to La Ville des Glaciers (Junction with the Day 3 route). Follow the Day 3 route to the Chalets des Mottets (1978m), (128).

Day 3 Les Chapieux – Elizabetta Hut (*A long ascent unfortunately accompanied by cars to La Ville des Glaciers.*)

Follow the road north-east past Seloge (133) to La Ville des Glaciers – which is a group of chalets! (Variant 2a joins here.) Descend east to the stream and rise north-east, crossing the Grand-Praz stream, to the Chalets des Mottets. Zig-zag up the shoulder above, leaving the Chalet de la Seigne path to the right, and then rise more gently to the wide Col de la Seigne (2516m).

Good views back and ahead with the first close glimpse of the southern side of Mont Blanc.

Descend easily north-east, probably over snow patches, cross a large stream and reach the Chalet Superieur de la Lex Blanche. Continue down and along the flat valley leading to the military ruins of the Lée Blanche. Go left and up to the Elizabetta Hut (119).

Day 4 Elizabetta Hut – Courmayeur (*This is certainly the day when the MBT makes the most of indifferent surroundings. Fortunately, the views of the Brouillard ridge on the Mont Blanc, the Dames Anglaises, the Aig. Noire de Peuterey and the Grandes Jorasses overshadow the ruined military buildings, huge moraines, dry lakes, tourists, cars and ski-lifts. The waymarking is poor so care is required in route-finding.*)

From the hut descend to the obvious track below, which leads east-north-east. Follow it, skirting the Lac Combal, to a point 50m before the bridge below the Lac du Miage, where there are red waymarks and a path ascending to the east (Variant 4a starts here). The path rises steeply past Alpe Inféreur de l'Arpvieille to the upper chalets of the same name (2303m). Go behind them and continue up, cross a ridge and then descend leaving the Col de Youla path to the right. Continue down north-east, past an insignificant lake, to the Lac Checroui (2165m). Still losing height and in the same direction reach the Col de Chécroui (1956m) (Variant 4b starts here). Descend west then north under a chair-lift and down a piste scar; a path once again leads beneath the Chalets de Peindein (127) to the road (Variant 4a joins here). Follow the road, past Notre-Dame de la Guérison, to Courmayeur (1224m) (118).

Bus-stop at the other side of the bridge for Courmayeur.

There are two GEs in the Chécroui area which seem of little use.

Day 4a Elizabetta Hut – Lavachey via Entreves (*This is useful if the weather is bad and follows unwaymarked road all the way to Lavachey (end of the Day 5 route). Unless one likes road-walking, this seems best done by bus via Courmayeur.*)

Follow the Day 4 route to the bridge and go down the road in the Val Veni, past Notre-Dame de la Guérison, to the valley above Courmayeur. Head north up a road which passes beneath the trunk road to Entrèves, through La Palud (129) (cable-cars to the Aig. du Midi) to Neyron. (Here Variant 5a can be reached by following a good path south-west signposted Bertone Hut and waymarked 25 in yellow.) More road (camp-sites, tennis courts and golf) leads to Lavachey (junction with the Day 5 route), (124).

Day 4b Elizabetta Hut – Courmayeur via Plan Chércroui (*The shortest way to Courmayeur.*)
Follow Day 4 to the Col Chécroui. Go east on a path waymarked by red crosses, via Pra-Neiron, Plan Chécroui and Dolonne, to Courmayeur.

The cable-car can be taken if desired.

Day 5 Courmayer – Lavachey
Follow road north-east out of Courmayeur to Villair Supérieur. Continue in the same direction up a good path, cross a stream, leave a path to the left and reach the junction (signpost) for the Bertone Hut (116). Follow the path in the valley, past La Trappe to Chapy. Head steeply in forest to a fine viewpoint called 'Pra Conduit' and continuing north-east Curru is soon reached (1964m, water). Rise steadily, sometimes over scree, cross another stream and zig-zag steeply to the Col Sapin (2436m). (Variant 5a joins here.) There are many paths in disarray descending east, choose the one that suits you. Contour the cwm, crossing numerous streams, and gain the obvious path above Alpe de Séchéron, which leads steeply to the Pas entre deux Sauts (2524m). Continue east to the path leading delightfully north above the valley bottom to the Alpe Supérieur de Malatra. There are paths all over the place formed by the cows and waymarking is poor. However, progress north-west to Malatra is easy and lower down the zig-zags in the forest lead to the valley (short-cuts). The path joins the road at a bus-stop, go left short-cutting the road twice to Lavachey (1642m), (Variant 4a joins here).

The waymarking takes the form of red lines or orange triangles.

Buses to Courmayeur.

Day 5a Courmayer – Lavachey via the Mont de la Saxe ridge (*This variant is far more worthwhile than the normal route. A 'must' if the weather is good.*)
Follow the normal route to the junction for the Bertone Hut. Go left and rise steeply to the hut situated at Le Pré. Still rising steeply north-east, gain the 'Mont de la Saxe ridge and follow indistinct paths to its highest point (2348m). Fine airy walking leads over the Tête Bernarda (2534m), down to a col, up over the Tête de la Tronche (2584m) and eventually down to the Col Sapin (junction with the Day 5 route which is followed to Lavachey).

Stupendous views all along.

From the ridge there is a 360° panorama. To the north the Grandes Jorasses (4208m) seem a stone's throw away. To the north-east is the Italian Val Ferret with the Petit and Grand cols at its head. To the east are the local peaks above Courmayeur. To the south are the Ruitor massif and the Graian Alps, and to the south-west, the Val Veni and the Col de la Seigne.

Day 6 Lavachey – La Fouly (*The Grand Col Ferret is on the Swiss-Italian frontier ridge. The walker descends into Switzerland and here various points should be noted. • Wild camping is forbidden in the Val Ferret, at Champex and the Val d'Arpette • Waymarking is excellent • Small signposts marked 'sentier de montagne' or 'tourisme pédestre' concern the MBT • Most services are expensive*)
From Lavachey retrace the route up the road and continue to the restaurant at Arnuva. Continue on road and then after 200m of track, the path leads to Pré de Bar then steeply passes some old chalets and climbs up to the Grand Col Ferret (2537m). Descend easily over pasture (favourite spot for baths and topless sunbathers) to La Peula. There is a choice of paths from here:

(a) Follow the jeep track (short-cuts) to the wooden bridge beneath Les Ars Dessous and then go up to the road which is subsequently followed to Ferret (120) and La Fouly (1610m), (123).

(b) Go left (north-west) and reach Le Clou (Variant 6a joins here)

More views of the same quality as the previous day except that the Swiss Alps are added in the forms Mont Vélan (3734m) and the Grand Combin (4314m). An ascent of the Tête de Ferret (2714m) provides a fine view of what is to come. From the foot of its south ridge a path traverses north-west towards the Petit Col Ferret.

From La Fouly. Buses to Praz-de-Fort or Orsières Tel. (026) 4.12.82.

via Planpro, follow the road to La Fouly.

Both paths are well waymarked.

Day 6a Lavachey – La Fouly via Petit Col Ferret (*An unfrequented and remote route, which will undoubtedly have snow on it until late in the season. The path is steep and sometimes bad. On the Swiss side the Combe des Fonds is exposed to ice and stonefall. It is, however, more direct than the normal route and can be reached from the Grand Col Ferret. Best reserved for good weather.*)

Follow the Day 6 route to a point just before Pré de Bar where a path goes north. Follow it, and then take another path which leaves the valley bottom heading up pasture and sometimes across deep gullies to the Petit Col Ferret (2490m). Descend to the north-east, in the Combe des Fonds, to the Crêtet de la Perche and a path leads north-east via La Léchère to Le Clou. Follow the road to La Fouly.

Day 7 La Fouly – Champex (*Most parties follow the road until reaching the path which rises to Champex, situated just after Issert. Although understandable, this is a pity. the MBT path down the superb Swiss Val Ferret attempts to show the walker just that little bit more. This day can comfortably be done in training shoes and is nice and short.*)

Go through La Neuva, which is really the La Fouly camp-site, on a good path. Cross the Reuse (local name for stream) de la Neuva, pass behind the hamlet of l'Amône and cross its stream, carry on north-east, crossing the Dranse de Ferret, and the Reuse de Planereuse. Following the former reach the Reuse de Saleina at Saleina d'Orsières. Go right to a road and go along it to Praz-de-Fort (1151m), (132). Take the road north out of the village, turn right into Les Arlaches and continue on a track to Issert. Continue through the village along the road to a signpost which shows the way to Champex. The path is easily followed in forest (it sometimes takes the form of a track) until it reaches the road just below Champex (1466m), (117). Follow it, passing the swimming-pool, and short-cut the two hairpins to the lake.

Champex is the Monte-Carlo of the MBT. the camp-site can be found at the far end of the resort.

Day 8 Champex – Col de la Forclaz

Take the road north-west out of Champex, leaving Variant 8a (signpost Val d'Arpette) to the left. Further on ignore a track on the left and continue to a signpost for the Sunways Hotel on the left, and follow the road to the hotel. Continue on the track which runs parallel to the stream, leave a concrete bridge to the left and go past the chalets of Champex d'en Bas to a junction. Go left, cross the bridge and reach Plan de l'Au (1330m). Rising steadily continue in forest to a point beneath the Chalet de la Jure and then zig-zag to the upper limit of the trees where the path traverses north then west to the Chalet de Bovine (1987m). Still heading west, drop steadily down to the Col de la Forclaz (1526m), (122).

D/R map wrong.

Day 8a Champex – Le Peuty via the Fenêtre d'Arpette (*This itinerary ought to be followed by Variant 9b, thus providing a magnificent outing. Instead of descending to Le Peuty, campers can use sites at Les Petoudes – very wild.*)

A signpost at the north-west exit of Champex indicates the road to be followed for Arpette (114). From there a track is easily followed south-west, occasionally waymarked, and then a path is taken on the

The final section is very steep, it may be snow-covered and will certainly have walkers knocking stones and blocks down. You should avoid them by keeping well to the left. The view north-west stretches from the Dents du Midi to

right (at a point where the trees begin to thicken), which leads to a small boulder-field (waymarks). Cross it, and when the path reappears climb to the junction with the Col des Ecandies. Go right and steeply but obviously to the Fenêtre d'Arpette (2671m). Dominating the Glacier de Trient, the path rapidly descends to the track above the Chalet de Vésevey (2096m). Drop down beneath it to the chalet and reach a path, which leads down, enters forest, and zig-zags to the ruined Chalet de l'Ourtié (1710m). Continue down to the snack-bar at the bridge and cross it (Variant 9b starts here). Follow the path signposted 'Trient' on the right (the usual black and yellow waymarks) which soon becomes a road and follow it down, past a barrier and gravel tips, to Le Peuty (1326m) (130), (junction with Day 9 and Variant 9a).

Day 9 and Variants 9a and 9b

The number of possibilities for continuing from Le Peuty, below the Col de la Forclaz, and the range of difficulty and quality call for a preliminary comment. The normal route to the Col de Balme provides very enjoyable walking with no particular difficulty, but the Col de Balme to Le Tour section is uninspiring – apart from the views of course. Variant 9a is not particularly good except for the section after Vallorcine. Variant 9b is the best way; for those on Variant 8a, it may seem a pity to have to head back up the valley but it is well worth the effort. The steep beginning of 9b is offset by the glacier scenery and the ensuing traverse, and the section to Tré-le-Champ via the Aiguillette des Posettes provides walking of the highest quality with excellent views all round.

Day 9   Col de la Forclaz – La Flégère

A signpost shows the way south, descend to Le Peuty (Variant 8a joins here), crossing the road once (1326m) (130). Go left on a track, over a bridge and rise steeply in forest. The path veers south-west to open ground ascending to Herbageres (2033m). Zig-zag steeply and then rise steadily to the old hotel at the Col de Balme (2191m), (115), (junction with Variant 9b). From behind the hut, walk easily down to the south-west alongside the ski-lifts to Le Tour (1463m), (134). Follow road to the SNCF station at Montroc-le-Planet (1354m), (126). Turn right and go over the railway through woodland and among chalets to the lower car-park at Tré-le-Champ-le-haut (1417m), (*113*), (135), (*126*), (junction with Variants 9a and 9b). A signpost indicates the way south-west and the path is easily followed among conifers providing unique views of the northern side of the Mont Blanc massif. Immediately after the Aiguillette d'Argentière, a fine pinnacle on the left of the path, climb steeply and enjoyably, using ladders and handrails for short stretches, to the huge cairn making the junction with Variant 9c and the path, which leads north to Lac Blanc. Descend to the Chalet des Chéserys (2005m) (a signpost points the way right of the building) and continue to La Flégère (1875m) (121).

Day 9a   Col de la Forclaz – La Flégère via Trient, Vallorcine and Tré-le-Champ-le-Haut

Follow the normal route to Le Peuty (junction with Variant 8a). Take a track north along the river to a bridge and go left between buildings (signpost). Rise steeply to Les Tseppes (1932m) and continue up round the ridge before heading south-west to the

Le Buet and, from a little higher up the Ecandies ridge, the Forbes Arête of the Aig. du Chardonnet (3824m) is visible as is the Aig. du Génépi (3265m). Looking towards the Swiss Alps, Mont Blanc de Cheilon (3869m), Pigne d'Arolla (3796m) and Dent Blanche (4356m) are easily recognisable.

In places minor land-slips will make the walking difficult.

Buses to Montroc and the rest of the Chamonix valley.

The ladder section requires no more than steadiness and a good head for heights. The Lac Blanc setting is probably the finest in the Aigs. Rouges. A hut and good paths heading south then south-west to rejoin the normal route just before La Flégère suffice in order to tempt the inquisitive.

buildings at Catogne (2011m). The MBT heads south (avoid continuing towards the Croix de Fer) and descends indistinctly to the
north-west to Les Lantses. Lower down a yellow signpost shows
the way to the Frontier Platform (a plateau the size of a football pitch
used by the Electricité de France). Go diagonally across beneath the
cable-car wires into forest, where French waymarks and signs
indicate the beginning of a fine path, which leads to Vallorcine
(1260m) (138). Continue south-west on a pleasant path alongside
the narrow-guage line, past Le Buet station and the Montets chapel,
over the Col des Montets (1461m), (Variant 9c leaves here), past a
car-park, to a lower one situated at Tré-le-Champ-le-haut. Follow
the Day 9 route to La Flégère.

Day 9b Le Peuty – La Flégère via Les Petoudes, Col de Balme,
Aiguillette des Posettes and Tre-le-Champ-le-haut

At Le Peuty, leave the MBT normal route to the right and follow a
road (the usual yellow and black waymarks), past gravel tips and a
barrier, then in zig-zags to a path, which leads to a bridge (junction
with Variant 8a, snack-bar). Rise steadily in forest and then over
more open ground to the ruins at Les Grands (wild camp pitch)
among superb glacier scenery. Traverse north-east, north-west,
then south-west to the Col de Balme across steep slopes (2191m)
(115), (junction with Day 9). There is a signpost north of the hotel.
Go west across the south flank of the Tête de Balme and then south
to the Col des Posettes (1997m). Reach the Aiguillette des Posettes
(2201m) either directly by the ridge or via the Chalets de Balme. Go
sou-sou-west and follow the magnificent ridge over the Tête de
Chenavier (1927m) down to a junction. Go either right or left, both
lead to Tré-le-Champ-le-haut (135). Follow Day 9.

*The south-east flank of the Aiguillette des Posettes is littered with
paths and signposts. Take a path according to your needs to Le
Tour – in case of an afternoon storm, the ridge is no place to be;
Montroc-le-Planet – transport and GE; Argentiere – provisions and
transport.*

Day 9c Col des Montets – Chalet des Chéserys (*This variation is
added for walkers who find scrambling awkward when laden and
who wish to avoid the ladder sections on Day 9.*)

From the Col des Montets a path leads south-west, then sou-sou-
west past Les Deviets to above the Chalet-des-Céserys. This can be
joined directly by a path which leaves the road above Tré-le-
Champ-le-haut on the left-hand side at the upper car-park.

Day 10 La Flégère – Les Houches

Go south-west and a stairway cut into the mountainside facilitates
progress before crossing pasture. Pass the ruined Chalet de
Charlanon to a short wooded section before rising steadily towards
the Planpraz ski networks. Avoiding the piste scars as much as
possible, zig-zag up to the old Hotel 2000. Behind it and to the right,
the path climbs steadily. Leave a path to the right before zig-
zagging to the Col du Brévent (2368m), (junction with GR5). From
the col traverse enjoyably among boulders and sometimes snow to
Le Brévent (2525m). From the summit continue south-west to the
Bellachat Hut (11). Descend steeply to the south-west to the zoo!
Follow the road west towards Le Coupeau and short-cut south to
the railway station at Les Houches (44), (*102*).

*Train to Montroc and the
rest of the Chamonix valley.*

*The summit of Le Buet
(3094m) is a magnificent
viewpoint – bear it in mind
for a future ascent.*

*At the Col des Montets, the
Aig. Rouges Nature Reserve
heralds a chalet which is
well worth a visit.*

*Escape to the south-east to
télécabine.*

Escape south to Le Tour.

*At La Flégère the prices may
be prohibitive and the hut
full. Ridiculous as it may
seem, under certain
circumstances it is financially
advantageous to descend to
the valley in the cable-car
(last car 17.30), camp at Les
Praz de Chamonix (131) and
return the following morning
(first car 7.45). With this in
mind one would not need to
carry the evening meal for
Day 9.*

*Commercial interests have
made a futile attempt at
making the slopes around
Planpraz skiable and in doing
so have desecrated the
area.*

*The views of the Rocher des
Fiz add to the magnificent
panorama of the Mont Blanc
range and its valley
stretching from the Aig. du
Bionnassay on the right to
the Aig. du Tour on the far
left.*

APPENDICES

1 TRANSPORT

GRANDE TRAVERSE

How to get to the starting points from Britain
Summer Train to Evian-les-Bains, then 'blue' buses to St. Gingolph. Plane to Geneva, then buses to St. Gingolph.
Winter Train or plane to Nice. Train to St. Dalmas de Tende (destination Coni-Cuneo, Italy), then by taxi or on foot to Les Mesches.

How to get back to Britain
Summer Train from Sospel or St. Dalmas de Tende to Nice. Train to Victoria, or plane to Heathrow, London.
Winter Buses from St. Gingolph to Evian-les-Bains, then train to either London or train to Geneva, then plane to London.

Note: A baggage limit of 20kg is imposed on those travelling by air.

The British Mountaineering Council Bus. Runs Mondays, Wednesdays and Fridays from London to Nice via Grenoble (allowing easy access to Briançon or Modane – Section C) and Fridays, Saturdays and Wednesdays from Nice to London. The service is operated by Wallace Arnold and offers highly competitive fares.

THE MONT BLANC TOUR

Les Houches, the departure and arrival point, is easily reached by train (SNCF) from Paris Gare de Lyon. It is situated on the narrow-guage line that links St. Gervais-le-Fayet to Martigny via the Chamonix valley. The Tour starts from the station itself and rises to the Col de Voza, which can be reached directly by tramway from St. Gervais.

For those travelling by air to Geneva, there is a coach link direct to Chamonix.

Coach services to Chamonix, via Geneva, are operated by Wallace Arnold for the British Mountaineering Council.

2 MAPS

WINTER   *SUMMER*

Section A   1.50 000 Didier/Richard Sheet:
                   Haut Pays Niçois
                   1.25 000 IGN Sheet 3841 ouest
                   1.25 000 IGN Sheet 3741 ouest

WINTER		SUMMER
Section B	1.50000 Didier/Richard Sheets:	
	Haut Pays Niçois	Section E
	Alpes de Provence	Section E
	Massifs du Queyras et Haute Ubaye	Section D
Section B	1.25000 IGN Sheet 3640 est	
Section C	1.50000 Didier/Richard Sheets:	
	Ecrins – Haut Dauphiné	Section D
	Massif et Parc National de la Vanoise	Section C
	Mont Blanc Beaufortain	
	1.25000 IGN Sheets:	
	Massif de la Vanoise Grande Casse/Dent Parrachée 236	
	Massif de la Vanoise Tarentaise 235	
	Massif du Mont Blanc Tré la Tête 232	
Section D	1.50000 Didier/Richard Sheets:	
	Mont Blanc Beaufortain	Section B
	Chablais, Faucigny et Genevois	Section A/B

The 1:25000 maps are included for their greater accuracy; they are not required in addition to the others for the summer traverse.

The best map for the Mont Blanc Tour is the D/R 1:50000 Mont Blanc Beaufortain.

These maps are available in Great Britain. They can be ordered through your local equipment specialist, or obtained from Stanfords, 12 Long Acre, London WC1. The maps are also available in France, particularly from Didier/Richard, 9 Grande Rue, 38000 Grenoble. IGN, 107, Rue la Boétie, 75008 Paris.

3 BIBLIOGRAPHY

Lac Léman/Col de la Cromix de Bonhomme; Haute Savoie. Ref. 504 GR5

Col de la Croix de Bonhomme/Modane; Parc National de la Vanoise; Savoie. Ref. 505 GR5/55

Modane à Larche; Savoie – Hautes-Alpes. Ref. 506 GR5

Larche/Nice; St. Dalmas-Valdeblore/Menton; Alpes de Haute Provence – Alpes-Maritimes. Ref. 507 GR5/52. Produced by the 'Féderation Française de la Randonnée Pedestre Comité National des Sentiers de Grande Randonnée (FFRP).

La Grande Traversée des Alpes. No. 15. Editions FAB and Co, Paris

Guide des Raids à Skis by Pierre Merlin. Denoël

Le Mercantour à Skis by Christian Boitel. Editions Serre

Avalanche – Proceedings of a Symposium for skiers, ski-mountaineers and mountaineers. Alpine Club, 74 South Audley Street, London W1Y 5FF

Official CAF Journals 'La Montagne et Alpinisme'. For the Mont Blanc Traverse – see 1981 No. 1

Avalanche Safety for Skiers and Climbers by Tony Daffern. Diadem Books, London

Tour du Mont Blanc Ref. 120 001 (FFRP)

4 ACCOMMODATION

The following list must be used in conjunction with the relevant text and the locality of a building is only given if it is *not* marked on the maps. Some of the information given is variable from one year to the next and each entry, in alphabetical order, has been checked with official sources.

The types of accommodation are categorized as follows with the abbreviations used in the list given in brackets:

Club Alpin Français (CAF), Club Alpin Italien (CAI) or Club Alpin Suisse (CAS) huts, where reduced rates for Alpine Club or Austrian Alpine Club members are obtainable. ● Park National de la Vanoise (PNV) huts. ● Privately owned hostels known as 'Gîtes d'Etape' (GE), where no more than two consecutive nights may be spent at a general unique tariff. ● Bivouacs (BV), in barns or ruins. ● Hotel (H). ● Camp-Sites (C-S).

Accommodation on the Grande Traverse
Club huts and Gîtes d'Etape, unless otherwise stated, are wardened from 15 June to 15 September and provide blankets, kitchen-ware and gas for cooking.

1 **Abriès** 1550m, small ski resort, Hs, GE open all year, Tel. 92.45.71.14, 50 beds, *Section B Winter, variant 12b.*
2 **Adus Hut** 2163m, CAF, burnt down in the summer of 1985. *Section E Summer, Day 31/Section A Winter, Day 4.*
3 **Agnel Hut** 2580m, Private, wardened Christmas period, 1 Feb. to 1 April, 60 beds, Tel. 92.45.83.90, *Section B Winter, Variant 12b.*
4 **Aiguilles** 1456m, resort with necessary facilities, GE open all year except April to June and October to December, Tel. 92.45.70.40, 26 beds, *Section B Winter, Day 13.*
5 **Alfred Wills Hut** 1897m, built on site of ruined 'Chalets d'Anterne', Private, unwardened but open in winter, Tel. 50.34.44.08, 65 beds, *Section B Summer, Day 5/Section D Winter, Day 27.*
6 **Auron** 1602m, Hs, restaurants, P.O., C-S – CAF hostel, Tel. 93.23.02.39, *Section E Summer, Day 27.*
7 **Aussois** 1483m, small ski resort, shops, *Section C Winter, Day 18.*
8 **Balme Hut** 2009m, Private, Tel. 79.55.70.62, 25 beds, *Section B Summer, Day 9.*
9 **Balme, Chalet-Hôtel de la** 1706m, Private, Tel. 50.47.03.54 closed in winter, beds, restaurant, *Section B Summer, Day 8/Section C Winter, Day 24/MBT Day 2.*
10 **Barenghi BV Hut** 2820m, CAI, keys available at Hotel de la Paix at Larche and from CAF huts at Maljasset and Chambeyron (also Fouillouze), 9 beds, two kitchens, small room left unlocked with 4 beds, *Section B Winter, Day 11.*
11 **Bellachat Hut** 2153m, Private, Tel. 50.53.46.99, 30 beds, *Section B Summer, Day 6/MBT Day 10.*
12 **Bellentre** 770m, hamlet, provisions, GE, *Section B Summer, Day 10.*
13 **Bellevue** 1786m, 2 Hs open all year, Tel. 50.93.48.18, *Section B Summer, Day 7/Section C Winter, Day 25/MBT Variant 1a.*
14 **Bionnassay** 1314m, hamlet, GE, Tel. 50.93.45.23, 44 beds, 12 if unwardened, *Section B Summer, Day 7/Section C Winter, Day 25/MBT Day 1.*
15 **Bise Hut** 1506m, CAF, Tel. 50.73.61.65, open all year, 70 beds, *Section A Summer, Day 1/Section D Winter, Day 32.*

16 **Blanche Hut** 2500m, CAF, wardened all year, *Section B Winter, Day 12.*
17 **Bois Hut** 1400m, PNV, Tel. 79.62.30.54, warden 20 December – 15 April, 65 beds, *Section C Winter, Day 20.*
18 **Bolline, La** 995m, village, Hs, provisions, *Section E Summer, Day 30.*
19 **Boréon, Chalet-Refuge du** 1580m, Private, Tel. 93.03.26.91, open all year, warden and restaurant service, 50 beds, *Section E Summer, Day 31/Section A Winter, Day 4.*
20 **Bossetan Hut** See Tornay.
21 **Bourg St. Maurice** 830m, large town providing all necessities inc. C–S, *Section C Winter, Day 22.*
22 **Bousiéyas** 1883m, GE, Tel. 93.02.42.08, open winter, restaurant service in summer, 16 beds, *Section E Summer, Day 25/Section B Winter, Day 9.*
23 **Briançon** 1290m, resort providing all necessities, Tourist Office 92.21.08.50 – GE, open all year, 45 beds, Tel. 92.21.28.93 at Le Fontenil, C–S, *Section D Summer, Day 18/Section B Winter, Day 14.*
24 **Brunissard** 1746m, village, GE open all year, 24 beds. Tel. 92.45.73.85, *Section D Summer, Day 19.*
25 **Ceillac** 1633m, small resort, H at l'Ochette, provisions – GE open all year, Tel. 92.45.00.23, 70 beds, C–S, *Section D Summer, Day 21.*
26 **Cervieres** 1636m, village – H, road link with Briançon – GE warden 15 Dec. – 20 April, Tel. 92.21.01.87, *Section B Winter, Day 14.*
27 **Chalp, La** 1680m, hamlet, GE/hotel, Tel. 92.45.72.89, 15 beds, *Section D Summer, Day 20.*
28 **Chambeyron Hut** 2626m, CAF, open all year, Tel. 92.81.04.73, 70 beds, no gas, no wood, warden in holiday period, *Section B Winter, Day 10.*
29 **Chamonix** 1020m, huge resort with every facility inc. C–S – GE 'Le Bois du Bouchet', Tel. 50.53.11.60, *Section B Summer, Day 6/Section D Winter, Day 25.*
30 **Chapelle d'Abondance, La** 1102m, small resort, H, shops, *Section A Summer, Day 1/Section D Winter, Day 31.*
31 **Chapieux, Les** 1540m, hamlet, provisions – H, Tel. 79.31.33.49 – GE, 10 beds, closed in winter – Nova Hut, Tel. 79.07.00.36, 41 beds, closed in winter, *Section B Summer, Day 8/Section C Winter, Day 24/MBT Day 2.*
32 **Chateau-Queyras** 1360m, Hs, restaurants, provisions – basic hostel in converted garage, ask at Grocers, Tel. 92.45.70.68, *Section D Summer, Day 20.*
33 **Châtel** 1150m, large resort, Hs, shops, C–S 'Le Loy, *Section A Summer, Day 2/Section D Winter, Day 30.*
34 **Col de la Vanoise Hut** (ex Félix-Faure) 2516m, CAF, wardened early April onwards, Tel. 79.08.25.23, 154 beds, 38 beds in winter, *Section C Summer, Day 13/Section C Winter, Day 19.*
35 **Col du Palet Hut** 2650m, PNV, Tel. 79.62.30.54, open in winter, 48 beds *Section C Summer, Day 12/Section C Winter, Day 20.*
36 **Contamines, Les** 1190m, small resort, Hs, restaurants, shops – CAF hut 'Le Nivorin', Tel. 50.47.00.88, open all year, warden 1 December to 1 May, *Section B Summer, Day 7/Section C Winter, Day 24/MBT Day 1.*
37 **Croix du Bonhomme Hut** 2443m, CAF, 20 beds, for winter telephone CAF Albertville 79.32.10.49, *Section B Summer, Day 8/Section C Winter, Day 24/MBT Day 2.*
38 **Dent Parrachée Hut** 2511m, CAF, Tel. 79.33.05.52, open all year, 29 beds, wood-stove, *Section C Winter, Day 18.*
39 **Félix-Faure** see Col de la Vanoise.
40 **Fonds, Les** 2040m, GE open all year, wardened holiday time, 9 beds, wood-stove, *Section B Winter, Day 14.*
41 **Fonts, Chalet des** 1349m, Private, Tel. 50.90.44.05, 35 beds, closed in winter, *Section B Summer, Day 5/Section D Winter, Day 27.*
42 **Fouillouze** 1907m, hamlet, GE, Tel. 92.84.31.16, open all year, 55 beds, *Section D Summer, Day 23/Section B Winter, Day 10.*
43 **Fruitière Hut** 1860m, Fontcouverte, Névache valley, Private, warden winter holiday time, 12 beds, *Section C Winter, Day 16.*
44 **Houches, Les** 993m, modern resort, Hs, restaurants, shops, C–S – GE at Les Chavants (1106m) open all year, Tel. 50.54.41.07, 140 beds, *Section B Summer, Day 7/Section C Winter, Day 25/MBT Days 1 and 10.*
45 **I re Magi Hut** 5 mins. on GR5 from Vallée Etroite hut, 1765m, warden Easter and Christmas, 75 beds, Tel. Italy code 39 (122) 96451, *Section D Summer, Day 16/Section C Winter, Day 16.*
46 **Isola 2000** Huge ski resort with every facility – CAF hut, 'Chastillon' near chapel, key needed, 12 beds, *Section A Winter, Day 5.*
47 **Lanches, Les** 1527m, summer C–S, *Section C Summer, Day 11.*
48 **Landry** 778m, Hs, provisions, C–S, *Section B Summer, Day 10.*

49 **Laquet Hut** Situated in France beneath Col de Coux – beds, *Section A Summer, Day 3/Section D Winter, Day 28.*

50 **Larche** 1670m, village, provisions, P.O., barns for BV, GE open all year, Tel. 92.84.30.80, 50 beds, *Section D Summer, Day 24/Section B Winter, Day 9.*

51 **Lay, Le** 1164m, hamlet, private hut, 20 beds, *Section B Summer, Day 7/MBT Day 1.*

52 **Leisse Hut** 2487m, PNV, Tel. 79.62.30.54, unwardened and open all year, *Section C Summer, Day 13.*

53 **Longon Hut** see Roure (Vacherie de)

54 **Madone de Fenestre Hut** 1903m, CAF, key needed in winter, Tel. 93.03.20.73, 62 beds, wood-stove, *Section E Summer, Day 32/Section A Winter, Day 3.*

55 **Maljasset Hut** 1910m, CAF, open and wardened all year, Tel. 92.84.31.15, 80 beds, *Section D Summer, Day 22/Section B Winter, Day 11.*

56 **Merveilles Hut** 2111m, CAF, Tel. 93.04.69.22, 85 beds, key needed in winter when unwardened, available at Gendarmerie St. Dalmas de Tende, wood-stove, *Section E Summer, Day 34/Section A Winter, Day 1.*
Day 15/Section C Winter, Day 17.

58 **Moëde-Anterne (Chalet-Cantine)** 1996m, Private, Tel. 50.93.60.43, closed in winter, *Section B Summer, Day 5/Section D Winter, Day 27.*

59 **Monta, La** 1660m, dGE, wardened 20 December to 30 April, 51 beds, restaurant service, Tel. 92.45.71.35, *Section B Winter, Variant 12b.*

60 **Montgenèvre** 1850m, large resort, Hs, shops, *Section C Winter, Variant 14a.*

61 **Morzine** 994m, modern resort with every facility inc. C–S, *Section A Summer, Day 3/Section D Winter, Day 28.*

62 **Motte, La** 2030m, Private Hut, 10 beds, unwardened, key available at c/o Mme. Emprin at Le Miroir (hamlet above St. Foy-en-Tarentaise), Tel. 79.08.11.20, *Secton C Winter, Day 22.*

63 **Nancroix** 1430m, small village, H, provisions, C–S, *Section C Summer, Day 11.*

64 **Nant Borrant Hut** 1390m, Private, 25 beds, must reserve in summer, Tel. 50.47.03.57, *Section B Summer, Day 8/Section C Winter, Day 24/MBT Day 2.*

65 **Neige et Merveilles** 1500m, Private, situated at La Miniere de Vallaure, Tel. 93.97.10.39, 200 beds, 10 beds in winter, *Section A Winter, Day 1.*

66 **Nevache** 1594m, hamlet, 4 GEs open all year, H, restaurant, P.O., provisions, restricted camping (ask at Mairie), *Section D Summer, Day 17/Section C Winter, Day 15.*

67 **Nice Hut** 2232m, CAF, 2 huts (both unwardened) – new summer hut, 60 beds, old hut, 25 beds, left open, wood-stove, warden holiday time – Tel. 93.04.62.74, *Section E Summer, Day 33/Section A Winter, Day 2.*

68 **Novel** 940m, small village, Hs – GE, Tel. 50.75.31.86, closed in winter, *Section A Summer, Day 1/Section D Winter, Day 32.*

69 **Orgère Hut** 1935m, PNV, Tel. 79.62.30.54, open all year, 80 beds, *Section C Summer, Day 15.*

70 **Pas, Le** 1280m, snacks available in summer, BV in winter, *Section A Summer, Day 3/Section D Winter, Day 28.*

71 **Péclet-Polset Hut** 2474m, CAF, open all year, Tel. 79.08.72.13, 70 beds, *Section C Summer, Day 14, (winter hut damaged).*

72 **Peisey-Nancroix** 1290m, village, Hs, restaurants, provisions, *Section C Summer, Day 11.*

73 **Pierre-Grosse** 1920m, GE, open all year but must reserve in winter, 25 beds, Tel. 92.45.81.28, *Section B Winter, Variant 13a.*

74 **Plaine-Dranse** 1660m, dormitory accommodation at bar-restaurant, open summer and winter, *Section A Summer, Day 2/Section D Winter, Day 29.*

75 **Plampinet** 1500m, GE, Tel. 92.21.32.48 or 21.13.22, 20 beds, open all year round, sleeping bag required, restaurant service, *Section C Winter, Variant 14a.*

76 **Planachaux (Switzerland)** 1860m, GE, Tel. (0250) 79.12.83, open all year, 70 beds, *Section A Summer, Day 3.*

77 **Plan de la Laie Hut** 1822m, CAF, open ski season, Tel. 79.32.10.49, Friday 18h00–20h00, 30 beds, wood-stove, *Section B Summer, Day 9/Section C Winter, Day 24.*

78 **Plan du Lac Hut** 2364m, PNV, Tel. 76.80.12.47 or Tel. 79.05.24.87, wardened at Easter, 30 beds, *Section C Winter, Variant 18b.*

79 **Plan Sec Hut** 2350m, situated east of, and 300m above, the Plan d'Amont dam, 2350m, private, warden all year, Tel. 79.05.22.88, 19 beds, *Section C Winter, Day 18.*

80 **Pralognon-La-Vanoise** 1424m, resort, Hs, restaurants, provisions, C–S, *Section C Summer, Day 14.*

81 **Presset Hut** 2514m, CAF, unwardened and open all year, Tel. 79.33.05.52, 22 beds, wood-stove, *Section B Summer, Day 9/Section C Winter, Day 23.*

82 **Rabuons Hut** 2523m, CAF, key available at 'Gendarmerie St. Sauveur s/Tinée in winter, 35 beds, wood-stove, *Section B Winter, Day 7.*

83 **Ricou Hut** 2040m, Private, Tel. 92.21.17.08, closed in winter, *Section C Winter, Day 16.*

84 **Rosuel Hut** 1556m, PNV, Tel. 79.62.30.54, 64 beds, central heating, showers, 7 beds in winter, *Section C Summer, Day 11/Section C Winter, Day 20.*

85 **Roure, Vacherie de** 1883m, situated north-east of Mt. Autcellier, Tel. 93.02.00.70, 32 beds, *Section E Summer, Day 28.*

86 **Roure (village)** 1096m, provisions – GE, key at 'Mairie', Tel. 93.02.00.37, 20 beds, *Section E Summer, Day 29.*

87 **Roya** 1500m, hamlet, GE open all year, Tel. 93.02.41.46, 32 beds, *Section E Summer, Day 27.*

88 **Ruitor Hut (Refuge de la Sassière)** 2030m, CAF, Tel. 79.32.10.49, 20 beds, unwardened, wood-stove, *Section C Winter, Variant 22a.*

89 **St. Dalmas de Tende** Arrival point or departure point for the traverses, see note at end of appendix, *Section E Summer, Variant 35a/Section A Winter, Day 0.*

90 **St. Dalmas-Le-Selvage** 1450m, Hs, restaurant, GE, *Section E Summer, Day 26.*

91 **St. Dalmas-Valdeblore** 1290m, Hs, restaurants, provisions, C–S – GE, open all year, Tel. 93.02.83.96, 32 beds, *Section E Summer, Day 30.*

92 **St. Etienne de Tinée** 1144m, Hs, restaurants, P.O., shops, clinic, C–S, *Section E Summer, Day 26.*

93 **St. Foy-en-Tarentaise** 1060m, hamlet, road link with Bourg St. Maurice, *Section C Winter, Day 22.*

94 **St. Gingolph** 380m, Frontier town, bus link, Hs, Departure point or arrival point for the traverses, *Section A Summer, Day 0/Section D Winter, Day 32.*

95 **St. Sauveur s/Tinée** 496m, Hs, restaurants, P.O., provisions, keys for CAF hut at Gendarmerie – GE, open and wardened all year, Tel. 93.02.01.58, 22 beds, *Section E Summer, Day 29.*

96 **St. Véran** 2011m, Europe's highest village, 2 GEs open all year, 'Pierre Belle', Tels. 92.45.81.39, 92.45.82.19, P.O., provisions, *Section B Winter, Day 12.*

97 **Salèse Hut** 1770m, Private, open if occupied, very basic, *Section E Summer, Day 31/Section A Winter, Day 4.*

98 **Samoëns** 699m, small resort, Hs, shops, *Section A Summer, Day 4/Section D Winter, Day 28.*

99 **Sixt** 756m, small resort, Hs, shops – GE (ask at Hôtel des Cimes), Tel. 50.90.44.22 – another GE at Salvagny, *Section   Summer, Day 4/Section D Winter, Day 27.*

100 **Sospel** 350m, small town, Hs, restaurants, provisions, P.O., C–S – GE at Place St. François, Tel. 93.04.00.09, 18 beds, *Section E Summer, Day 36.*

101 **Stroppia Hut** 2100m, CAI, very difficult access, key available at Larche, *Section B Winter, Day 11.*

102 **Taconnaz (les Houches)** 1014m, GE, Tel. 50.54.43.28, 52 beds, warden Easter–September, *Section B Summer, Days 6 and 7/Section C Winter, Day 25/MBT Days 1 and 10.*

103 **Thabor Hut** 2470m, CAF, situated near Lacs Ste. Marguerite, 52 beds, Tel. 79.05.22.13, wardened 22 March – 19 May, *Section D Summer, Day 16/Section C Winter, Day 17.*

104 **Tignes** 1800m, small hamlet, *Section C Winter, Day 21.*

105 **Tignes, Le Lac de** 2083m, modern ski resort, Hs, BV disapproved of – CAF hostel open all year except June, Tel. 79.06.31.56, 80 beds, *Section C Winter, Day 20.*

106 **Tornay Hut (Bossetan Hut)** 1763m, CAF, open all year, Tel. 50.90.10.94, 40 beds, *Section A Summer, Day 4/Section D Winter, Day 28.*

107 **Val Claret** 2120m, ski resort, mostly Hs and flats, shops, *Section C Summer, Day 12/Section C Winter, Day 20.*

108 **Valezan** 1200m, hamlet, GE, *Section B Summer, Day 10.*

109 **Vallée Etroite Hut** 1769m, CAI, Tel. Italy code 39 11.54.60.31, 40 beds, *Section D Summer, Day 16/Section C Winter, Day 16.*

110 **Vens Hut** 2370m, CAF, key needed (for availability see Rabuons Hut), sometimes open in winter, 36 beds, wood-stove, *Section B Winter, Day 8.*

111 **Vigny** 1461m, Private, probably closed, 20 beds, Tel. 50.79.14.86, *Section A Summer, Day 3/Section D Winter, Day 28.*

112 **Villard St. Pancrace** small village, GE, open all year, 40 beds, *Section B Winter, Variant 12a.*

Note For parties starting or finishing the traverses at St. Dalmas de Tende the GE at Tende (4km up the valley) will provide friendly accommodation at special rates and any necessary information in English (local snow conditions for example). Transport to Les Mesches and, if desired, a guide for a part of whole of the traverse are available.

Accommodation on the Mont Blanc Tour • There are some local restrictions on camping, which should be respected – mention of these is made in the text. • The Swiss concept of a Gîte d'Etape is not the same as in France, they are more luxurious and prices are not standardized. • For those sections of the Tour that are common with the Summer Traverse, the accommodation entries are given in the main body of this appendix. • The accommodation outside France is given by the abbreviations I (Italy) and Sz (Switzerland).

113 **Argentière** 1500m, resort with necessary facilities, C–S – 2 private huts, Le Nouveau Grassonet, Tel. 50.54.01.87 and Chalet-Ref. de l'Essarton at C–S, Tel. 50.54.03.08, *Day 9.*
114 **Arpette** (Sz) 1688m, 2 chalets – private hut, Tel. (026) 54.12.21 – C–S, *Variant 8a.*
115 **Balme Hôtel** 2191m, private hut, *Day 9.*
116 **Bertone Hut** (I) 2000m, private, 40 beds, Tel. (0165) 84.38.91. *Variant 5a.*
117 **Champex** (Sz) 1466m, private huts, Belvédère, Tel (026) 4.11.14, Plien-Air, 60 beds, Tel. (26) 4.23.50 – CAS Hotel, 14 beds, Tel. (026) 4.11.61 – C–S, provisions, Hs. At Champex d'en Haut, C–S, restaurant, provisions, Youth Hostel, Tel. (26) 4.14.23, *Day 7.*
118 **Courmayeur** (I) 1224m, large resort with every facility, buses to Chamonix via Mont Blanc tunnel, *Day 4.*
119 **Elizabetta Hut** (I) 2300m, CAI, 66 beds, Tel. (0165) 84.37.43, *Day 3.*
120 **Ferret** (Sz) 1705m, hamlet, H, private hut, 26 beds, Tel. (026) 4.11.88, *Day 6.*
121 **La Flégère** 1875m, cable-car station, private hut, 100 beds, restaurant, *Day 9.*
122 **Forclaz, Col de la** (Sz) 1526m, hotel-cum-hut, Tel. (026) 2.26.88, *Day 8.*
123 **Fouly, La** (Sz) 1610m, village resort, shops, Edelweiss Hut, private, 40 beds, Tel. (026) 4.26.21, C–S, *Day 6.*
124 **Lavachey** (I) 1730m, hamlet, 2 huts, 80 beds, Tel. (0165) 89.99.7, *Day 5/Variant 4a.*
125 **Miage Hut** 1560m, private, 20 beds, Tel. 50.78.07.16, *Variant 1a.*
126 **Montroc-le Planet** 1354m, village, GE at station, *Day 9.*
127 **Monte-Bianco Hut** (I) 1666m, wardened 27 June – 7 August, 100 beds, Tel. (021) 49.984, *Day 4.*
128 **Mottets, Chalets des** 1864m, private hut, 60 beds, Tel. 79.00.01.90, *Day 3/Variant 2a.*
129 **Palud, La** (I) 1350m, cable-car station, shops, *Variant 4a.*
130 **Peuty, Le** (Sz) 1326m, GE, 50 beds, Tel. (026) 2.23.97, C–S ask at GE, *Day 9/Variant 8a.*
131 **Praz de Chamonix, Les** 1060m, village, shops, C–S, cable-car for La Flégère, *Day 9.*
132 **Praz-de-Fort** (Sz) 1151m, hotel-cum-hut, Tel. (26) 54.11.68, provisions, *Day 7.*
133 **Seloge** 1809m, hamlet, GE, 48 beds, restaurant, provisions, *Day 3.*
134 **Tour, Le** 1470m, village, CAF hut, 15 beds, Tel. 50.54.04.16, *Day 9.*
135 **Tre-le-Champ** 1400m, group of chalets, GE, 20 beds, Tel. 50.54.05.14, *Day 9.*
136 **Trient** (Sz) 1320m, hamlet, H, GE, *Variant 9a.*
137 **Truc Hut** 1750m, private, 30 beds, Tel. 50.93.12.48, *Variant 1a.*
138 **Vallorcine** 1260m, village, shops, GE and C–S at Les Plans, 20 beds, Tel. 50.54.61.77, *Variant 9a.*